Floral
Knitting

Floral
Knitting

Susan Duckworth

Photography by Sandra Lousada

Trafalgar Square Publishing
NORTH POMFRET, VERMONT

Editor: Sandy Carr
Design: Patrick McLeavey
Pattern Checker: Marilyn Wilson
Stylist: Lottie Johansson
Hair and Makeup: Barbara Jones from Artistic Licence
Transport: Nick from Roger Royce with Dog George
Assistants to Sandra Lousada: Rebecca Lacy, Lucy Tizara
Charts: Dennis Hawkins
Illustrations: Connie Jude

Text and Original designs copyright © Susan Duckworth 1991
Photographs copyright © Century 1991

First published in the United States of America in 1992
by Trafalgar Square Publishing, North Pomfret, Vermont 05053

Originally published in Great Britain by Century Editions,
an imprint of the Random Century Group Ltd,
20 Vauxhall Bridge Road, London SW1V 2SA

LOC 91–65582

Typeset by SX Composing Ltd, Rayleigh, Essex, UK

Printed and bound in Singapore

ISBN 0 943955 47 5

Note: The patterns in this book may not be knitted for resale.

Contents

Introduction

I never grow tired of floral patterns. Although countless varieties of colour designs have been used on knitting – from the traditional Fair Isles to picture sweaters – flower patterns are my favourites.

I love to work in my garden all year round. I'm in daily touch with it – planting, planning, inspecting tending, and I'm sure the joy I get from it must be reflected in my knitting designs. In fact, I cannot devote as much time to my garden as I would really like, as knitting design is also a time-consuming and absorbing occupation – so I work between the two, which is a perfect combination.

It was a natural step for me to design a collection around a floral theme – using flowers in their many forms – and it's been interesting to see just which flowers really lend themselves to being knitted. I like to work with fairly fine yarns but, even so, you are quite limited by the tension – in 4 ply around 3 stitches to the centimetre (7 stitches to the inch). The makers of Persian carpets, for example, could have over 10 times as many knots in their designs, which gives a lot more scope for rich and intricate detail. Some of my favourite flowers, such as snake's head fritillary, bearded iris, hellebores and auriculas, have proved quite a challenge, and I've had to abandon my efforts sometimes, as the images produced were not strong enough.

Mostly I like to work direct from the flowers themselves, first drawing them, then transferring them to graph paper, simplifying the shapes and knitting up swatches to balance the colours. I prefer working from life to taking designs from historic embroideries and textiles. Occasionally I do use these wonderful designs as a source of inspiration but then I have to transform them into something new, rather than use them exactly as they are.

Of course, this process is very time-consuming, but it always seems worthwhile as hand-knitting has a particular charm all its own. Sometimes I will get quite carried away with a really intricate idea, though these very complicated swatches rarely end up as finished sweaters – it would be too cruel to expect my team of excellent knitters to cope with such designs. I keep the ideas for my own pleasure and possibly as a reference for some future simpler treatment.

I do like to work with lots of yarns, and to introduce textured stitches among the areas of flat colour, but there is a wide range of patterns in the book to suit all levels of knitter. The children's designs, in particular, are quite easy, with fewer colours and less intricate patterning. Designs like Chevron Floral, Tartan Flower and Tapestry will be really quite challenging to knit.

More and more I like to work on designs that are completely one-off – that just cannot be duplicated. The collage sweater I'm wearing in the picture opposite is just such a design. (My daughter is wearing the Cloche on page 129 and a version of the Chevron Floral sweater on page 94.) I made it by assembling lots of swatches I'd produced while trying out ideas for other sweaters; you could do the same thing using tension swatches. This way no two garments would ever be the same.

If you want to, you can reproduce the designs in this book more or less exactly, by knitting them in the original colours I used (these are listed on page 140). To make it easier for you, there are yarn kits available for all the main colourways. But if you use your own colours, it will not only be cheaper, because in many cases you will be able to use up some of your oddments of leftover yarns from previous projects, but you will also be producing something really unique.

Happy knitting!

Susan M. Duckworth

Summer
Season

Oriental Poppies

These blowsy poppies – copied from an old seed packet – are worked in a mixture of silky yarns and soft wools on a creamy cabled background. I've done this design in a number of colourways – pages 15 and 54, for instance.

SIZE
To fit one size only up to 96cm (38in) bust
Actual width measurement 106cm (41¾in)
Length to shoulder 64.5cm (24¼in)
Sleeve seam 47cm (18½in)

MATERIALS
400g (16oz) four-ply yarn in main colour (A)
25g (1oz) in each of 13 contrast colours
   (B, C, D, E, F, G, H, J, L, M, N, Q, R)
1 pair each 3mm (US2) and 3¼mm (US3) needles
Cable needle
2.50mm (USC) crochet hook

TENSION
26 sts and 36 rows to 10cm (4in) over st st on 3¼mm (US3) needles

SPECIAL ABBREVIATIONS
cross 4 left – sl 3 sts on to cable needle, hold at front, P1, K3 from cable needle
cross 4 right – sl 1 st on to cable needle, hold at back, K3, P1 from cable needle
cross 5 left – sl 3 sts on to cable needle, hold at front, P2, K3 from cable needle
cross 5 right – sl 2 sts on to cable needle, hold at back, K3, P2 from cable needle
cable 6 back – sl 3 sts on to cable needle, hold at back, K3, K3 from cable needle

(Opposite) The early evening light catches the texture of the cables and the bright glowing tones of the poppies in this classic cardigan.

BACK
Using 3mm (US2) needles and yarn A, cast on 160 sts. Work 6cm (2¼in) in K1, P1 rib, ending with a rs row. Change to 3¼mm (US3) needles and commence cable patt:

1st row (ws) K1, P1, *work 1st row of chart 1*, K2, rep from * to * to last 23 sts, K2, rep from * to * again, P1, K1.
2nd row P1, K1, * work 2nd row of chart 1*, P2, rep from * to * to last 23 sts, P2, rep from * to * again, K1, P1.
These 2 rows establish the cable patt. Cont as set until 29 rows have been worked from chart 1, ending with a ws row.
Now cont in flower patt from charts 2 and 3, *at the same time* keeping cable patt worked from chart 1 correct; use separate lengths of yarn for each colour area and twist yarns tog at colour joins to avoid holes.
1st row (rs) P1A, K1A, work 30th row of chart 1, P2A, work 30th row of chart 1, K1A, work 1st row of chart 2, K4A, work 30th row of chart 1, K2A, work 1st row of chart 1, K5A, work 1st row of chart 1, K1A, P1A.
2nd row K1A, P1A, work 31st row of chart 1, P5A, work 2nd row of chart 2, P2A, work 31st row of chart 1, P4A, work 2nd row of chart 2, P1A, work 31st row of chart 1, P2A, work 31st row of chart 1, P1A, K1A.
3rd-37th rows Cont as set, keeping chart 1 correct, until 37 rows have been worked from chart 2, ending with a rs row.
38th row (ws) K1, P1, work 3rd row of chart 1, P16, work 1st row of chart 3, P28, work 1st row of chart 3, P10, work 3rd row of chart 1, P1, K1.
39th row P1, K1, work 4th row of chart 1, K10, work 2nd row of chart 3, K28, work 2nd row of chart 3, K16, work 4th row of chart 1, K1, P1.
40th-72nd rows Cont as set, keeping chart 1 correct, until 35 rows have been worked from chart 3.

□ = using A, K on rs rows,
    P on ws rows
⊡ = using A, P on rs rows,
    K on ws rows
⬒⬓⬔⬕ = cable 6 back
⬓⬔⬕ = cross 5 right
◻◻◻ = cross 4 left
◻◻◻◻ = cross 5 left
◻◻◻ = cross 4 right

work charts 2 and 3
in st st only

□ = A		⊞ = H	
◉ = B		⬭ = J	
◪ = C		⊡ = L	
⊠ = D		⊟ = M	
◼ = E		⊡ = N	
◣ = F		◩ = Q	
◥ = G		◲ = R	

CHART 1

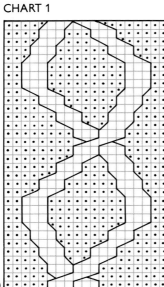

1st row (ws)

CHART 2

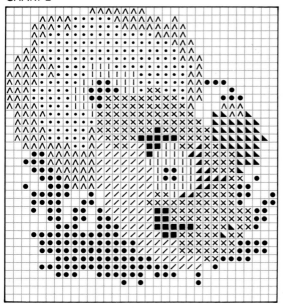

The last 72 rows form the flower patt, noting always to keep chart I correct. Cont as set until 104 rows have been worked in flower patt.

Shape armholes
Cast off 7 sts at beg of next 4 rows. 132 sts.
Cont without shaping, ceasing to work chart I at armhole edges, until 174 rows have been worked in flower patt.

Shape shoulders
Cast off 14 sts at beg of next 4 rows and 13 sts at beg of foll 2 rows.
Cast off rem 50 sts.

LEFT FRONT
**Using 3mm needles and yarn A, cast on 81 sts.
Work in KI, PI rib as foll:
1st row (rs) KI, (PI, KI) to end.
2nd row PI, (KI, PI) to end
Rep the last 2 rows until work measures 6cm (2¼in) from cast-on edge, ending with a rs row.**
Commence cable patt:
1st row (ws) P3A, *work 1st row of chart I, rep from * to last 2 sts, PIA, KIA.
2nd row PIA, KIA, *work 2nd row of chart I, rep from * to last 3 sts, K3A.
These 2 rows establish the cable patt. Cont as set until 29 rows have been worked from chart I.
Now commence flower patt from charts 2 and 3, *at the same time* keeping chart I correct, as foll:
1st row (rs) PIA, KIA, *work 30th row of chart I, rep from * to last 41 sts, K3A, work 1st row of chart 2, K5A.
2nd row P5A, work 2nd row of chart 2, P3A, *work 31st row of chart I,, rep from * to last 2 sts, PIA, KIA.
3rd-37th rows Cont as set until 37 rows have been worked from chart 2.
38th row (ws) P3A, work 3rd row of chart I, work 1st row of chart 3, P6A, work 3rd row of chart I, PIA, KIA.
39th row PIA, KIA, work 4th row of chart I, K6A, work 2nd row of chart 3, work 4th row of chart I, K3A.
40th-72nd rows Cont as set, keeping chart I correct, until 35 rows have been worked from chart 3.
The last 72 rows form the flower patt, noting always to keep chart I correct. Cont as set until 104 rows have been worked in flower patt.

Shape armhole
Cast off 7 sts at beg of next and foll alt row. 67 sts.
Now cont without shaping, ceasing to work chart I at armhole edge, until front measures 15 rows less than back to shoulder shaping, ending at front edge.

Shape neck
Cast off 8 sts at beg of next row and 4 sts at beg of 2 foll alt rows. Now dec 1 st at neck edge on every row until 41 sts rem, ending at armhole edge.

Shape shoulder
Cast off 14 sts at beg of next and foll alt row.
Work 1 row. Cast off rem 13 sts.

RIGHT FRONT
Work as for left front from ** to **.
Commence cable patt:
1st row (ws) KIA, PIA, *work 1st row of chart I, rep from * to last 3 sts, P3A.
2nd row K3A, *work 2nd row of chart I, rep from * to last 2 sts, KIA, PIA.
These 2 rows establish the cable patt. Cont as set until 29 rows have been worked from chart I.
Now commence flower patt from charts 2 and 3, *at the same time* keeping chart I correct, as foll:
1st row (rs) K5A, work 1st row of chart 2, K3A, *work 30th row of chart I, rep from * to last 2 sts, KIA, PIA.
2nd row KIA, PIA, *work 31st row of chart I, rep from * to last 41 sts, P3A, work 2nd row of chart 2, P5A.
3rd-37th rows Cont as set until 37 rows have been worked from chart 2.
38th row (ws) KIA, PIA, work 3rd row of chart I, P6A, work 1st row of chart 3, work 3rd row of chart I, P3A.
39th row (rs) K3A, work 4th row of chart I, work 2nd row of chart 3, K6A, work 4th row of chart I, KIA, PIA.
40th-72nd rows Cont as set, keeping chart I correct, until 35 rows have been worked from chart 3.
The last 72 rows form the flower patt, noting always to keep chart I correct.
Complete to match left front, reversing all shapings.

SLEEVES
Using 3mm (US2) needles and yarn A, cast on 51 sts. Work 9cm (3½in) in KI, PI rib as given for left front, ending with a ws row.
Inc row Rib 5, (inc 1 in next st, rib 7) to last 6 sts, inc 1 in next st, rib 5. 57 sts.
Rib 1 row
Inc row (K twice into next st, KI) to last st, K twice into last st. 86 sts.
Change to 3¼mm (US3) needles. Commence cable patt:
1st row (ws) (K2, work 1st row of chart I) to last 2 sts, K2.
2nd row (P2, work 2nd row of chart I) to last 2 sts, P2.
These 2 rows establish the cable patt. Cont as set until 64 rows have been worked in cable patt, *at the same time* inc and work into reverse st st 1 st at each end of 4th and every foll 6th row. 108 sts.
Now commence flower and cable patt:
Next row P30A, work 1st row of chart 2, P2A, work 1st row of chart I, P24A.
Next row K24A, work 2nd row of chart I, K2A, work 2nd row of chart 2, K30A.
These 2 rows establish the patt. Cont as set until 37 rows have been worked from chart 2, *at the same time* keep chart I correct and inc and work into st st 1 st at each end of every foll 6th row as before. 120 sts.
Commence flower patt:

work charts 2 and 3 in st st only

□ = A	⊞ = H
⊡ = B	⊠ = J
◪ = C	⊡ = L
⊠ = D	⊟ = M
■ = E	⊡ = N
◣ = F	◩ = Q
◪ = G	◪ = R

CHART 3

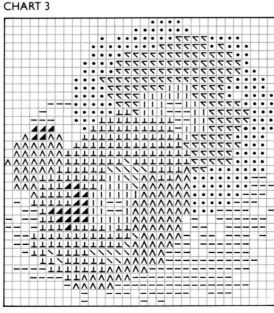

Next row (rs) K38A, work 1st row of chart 3, K50A.

This row establishes position of chart 3.

Cont as set, inc and work into st st 1 st at each end of every 6th row as before until there are 126 sts. Then cont without further shaping until 35 rows have been worked from chart 3.

Cont in yarn A only.

Work 6 rows st st.

Commence central cable patt:

Next row (ws) P44A, (work 1st row of chart 1) twice, P44A.

This row establishes the position of chart 1, with st st edge sts.

Shape sleeve top

Keeping patt as now set, cast off 7 sts at beg of next 4 rows.

Dec 1 st at each end of next and every foll alt row until 52 sts rem, ending with a ws row. Cast off 8 sts at beg of next 4 rows.

Cast off rem 20 sts.

BUTTON BAND

Using 3mm (US2) needles and yarn A, cast on 9 sts. Work in rib as given for left front until band, when slightly stretched, fits up left front to neck shaping.

Cast off in rib.

Place 12 button markers on button band, the first 4 rows from cast-on edge, the last 6 rows from cast-off edge, with rem 10 evenly spaced between.

BUTTONHOLE BAND

Work to match button band, making buttonholes opposite button markers as foll:

1st buttonhole row Rib 3, cast off 3, rib to end.

2nd buttonhole row Rib to end, casting on 3 sts over those cast off in previous row.

COLLAR

Using 3mm (US2) needles and yarn A, cast on 142 sts. Work 6 rows K1, P1 rib.

Cont in rib, dec 1 st at each end of next and 6 foll alt rows. Work 1 row.

Cast off 4 sts at beg of next 4 rows. Cast off rem 112 sts.

TO MAKE UP

Join shoulder seams. Set in sleeves, easing fullness over shoulder.

Join side and sleeve seams.

Sew on front bands.

Sew collar to neck edge, beg and end at inner edges of front bands.

Collar edging

Using 2.50mm (USC) crochet hook and yarn A, work crochet picot edging as foll:

1st row Work in double crochet around collar edge.

2nd row *Work 1 double crochet into each of next 3 double crochet, 4 chain, slip st into last double crochet; rep from *.

Sew on buttons.

Oriental Poppies on an indigo background (right); and the Wavy Fair Isle sweater (centre, page 50) and the Auriculas sweater (left, page 84) both worn oversized by children.

Anemones

Anemones really are my favourite flower. I love their distinctive black centres surrounded by blue-reds, purples and Bengal pinks. There are two versions of the design. The black on page 21 is a short jacket with a shawl collar worked in moss stitch. The cream colourway is a V-necked cardigan with a narrow vertical stripe in smoky grey worked on the background colour. There is also a black version of the vertical-striped cardigan.

CARDIGAN

SIZE
To fit one size only up to 91cm (36in) bust
Actual width measurement 98.5cm (38¾in)
Length to shoulder 62cm (24¼in)
Sleeve seam 48.5cm (19in)

MATERIALS
450g (18oz) 4-ply in main colour (A)
50g (2oz) in each of 4 contrast colours
   (B, C, H, L)
25g (1oz) in each of 13 contrast colours
   (D, E, F, G, J, M, N, Q, R, S, T, U, V)
1 pair each 2¾mm (US2) and 3mm (US2) needles
9 buttons

TENSION
35 sts and 37 rows to 10cm (4in) over chart patt on 3mm (US2) needles.

BACK
Using 2¾mm (US2) needles and yarn A, cast on 168 sts.
Work in striped rib as foll:
1st row (rs) (K1A, K1B, K1A, P2A) to last 3 sts, K1A, K1B, K1A.
2nd row (P1A, P1B, P1A, K2A) to last 3 sts, P1A, P1B, P1A.
These 2 rows form the striped rib.
Rep them 7 times more, dec 1 st at end of last row. 167 sts.
Change to 3mm (US2) needles and beg colour patt from chart on page 18, working in st st throughout between back markers; use separate lengths of yarn for each colour area and twist yarns tog at colour joins to avoid holes.
Work 96 rows of chart, then rep 33rd-96th rows until work measures 42cm (16½in) from cast-on edge, ending with a ws row.
Shape armholes
Cast off 7 sts at beg of next 2 rows. Dec 1 st at each end of next and every foll alt row until 149 sts rem.
Now work straight until back measures 20cm (7¾in) from beg of armhole shaping, ending with a ws row.

These richly coloured bunches of anemones make a cool cotton summery cardigan.

CARDIGAN CHART

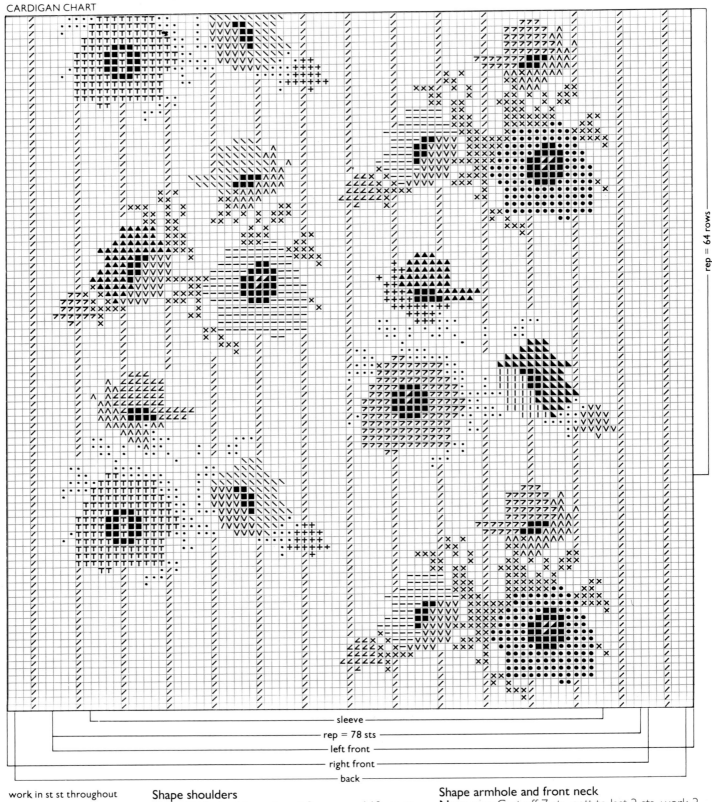

rep = 64 rows

sleeve
rep = 78 sts
left front
right front
back

work in st st throughout

□ = A		⊞ = N	
◪ = B		◭ = Q	
⊠ = C		◪ = R	
◉ = D		◩ = S	
◩ = E		◼ = T	
◪ = F		⊓ = U	
⊟ = G		◭ = V	
◼ = H			
◪ = J			
⊡ = L			
⊓ = M			

Shape shoulders
Cast off 16 sts at beg of next 2 rows and 18 sts at beg of next 4 rows. 45 sts.
Cast off.

RIGHT FRONT
Using 2¾mm (US2) needles and yarn A, cast on 83 sts. Work 16 rows in striped rib as given for back, inc 1 st at each end of last row. 85 sts.
Change to 3mm (US2) needles and work in colour patt from chart between right front markers. Work 96 rows of chart, then rep 33rd-96th rows until right front matches back to armhole, ending at side edge.

Shape armhole and front neck
Next row Cast off 7 sts, patt to last 2 sts, work 2 tog.
Keeping patt correct, dec 1 st at armhole edge on next and foll alt row, *at the same time* dec 1 st at neck edge on every foll 3rd and alt row alternately until 52 sts rem.
Now work straight until right front matches back to shoulder, ending at armhole edge.
Shape shoulder
Cast off 16 sts at beg of next row and 18 sts at beg of foll alt row.
Work 1 row.
Cast off rem 18 sts.

LEFT FRONT
Work as given for right front, working from chart between left front markers and reversing all shapings.

SLEEVES
Using 2¾mm (US2) and yarn A, cast on 68 sts.
Work 5cm (2in) in K1, P1 rib, ending with a ws row.
Now work 26 rows in striped rib as given for back.
Change to 3mm (US2) needles and work in colour patt from chart between sleeve markers, *at the same time* inc and work into patt 1 st at each end of every foll 3rd row until there are 78 sts. Now cont inc as before, working extra sts into stripes of A and B as set, until there are 138 sts (work 96 rows of chart, then rep 33rd-96th rows).
Cont straight until work measures 48.5cm (19in) from beg, ending with a ws row.
Cast off.

FRONT BAND
Join shoulder seams.
Using 2¾mm (US2) needles and yarn A, cast on 11 sts.
1st row (rs) K1, (P1, K1) to end.
2nd row P1, (K1, P1) to end.
Rep last 2 rows until band, when slightly stretched, fits up left front to beg of neck shaping. Place 9 button markers on left front band, one 2cm (¾in) from cast-on edge and one at beg of neck shaping, and the rest spaced evenly between.
Cont in K1, P1 rib until band when slightly stretched, fits up left front neck, around back neck and down right front edge, *at the same time* making buttonholes to correspond with button markers as foll:
1st buttonhole row (rs) Rib 4, cast off 3 sts, rib to end.
2nd buttonhole row Rib to end, casting on 3 sts over those cast off in previous row.
Cast off in rib.

TO MAKE UP
Join on front band. Set in sleeves, sewing cast-off edge around entire armhole.
Join side and sleeve seams. Sew on buttons.

A sleeve detail from the cream colourway of the Anemones cardigan.

JACKET

SIZE
To fit one size only up to 97cm (38in) bust
Actual width measurement 108.5cm (42¾in)
Length to shoulder 55cm (21½in)
Sleeve 43cm (17in)

MATERIALS
400g (16oz) 4-ply in main colour (A)
75g (3oz) in 1 contrast colour (L)
50g (2oz) in each of 2 contrast colours (J, Q)
25g (1oz) in each of 13 contrast colours
  (B, C, D, E, F, G, H, M, N, R, S, T, U)
1 pair each 2¾mm (US2) and 3mm (US2) needles
3mm (US2) circular needle
7 buttons

TENSION
33 sts and 37 rows to 10cm (4in) over chart patt on 3mm (US2) needles.

BACK
Using 2¾mm (US2) needles and yarn A, cast on 176 sts. Work 16 rows in K1, P1 rib.
Change to 3mm (US2) needles and beg colour patt from chart on page 20 working in st st throughout; use separate lengths of yarn for each colour area and twist yarns tog at colour joins to avoid holes.
1st row (rs) (K1A, P4A) twice, (work 1st row of chart) twice, (P4A, K1A) twice.
2nd row (P1A, K4A) twice, (work 2nd row of chart) twice, (K4A, P1A) twice.
These 2 rows establish the position of chart with edge sts in rib. Work 134 rows of chart then rep 71st-134th rows to form patt until work measures 36cm (14in) from cast-on edge, end with ws row.
Shape armholes
Cast off 7 sts at beg of next 4 rows. Dec 1 st at each end of next and every foll alt row until 134 sts rem. Now work straight until back measures 19cm (7½in) from beg of armhole shaping, ending with a ws row.
Shape shoulders
Cast off 15 sts at beg of next 6 rows. 44 sts.
Cast off.

(Left) This is a detail from the Anemones cardigan worked in wool with a black and sage striped background.

JACKET CHART

□ = A
■ = A
⊠ = B
⊟ = C
⊡ = D
▲ = E
▼ = F
◩ = G
◉ = H
◪ = J
◭ = L
◿ = M
⊡ = N
⬓ = Q
⊞ = R
⬔ = S
⬚ = T
◪ = U

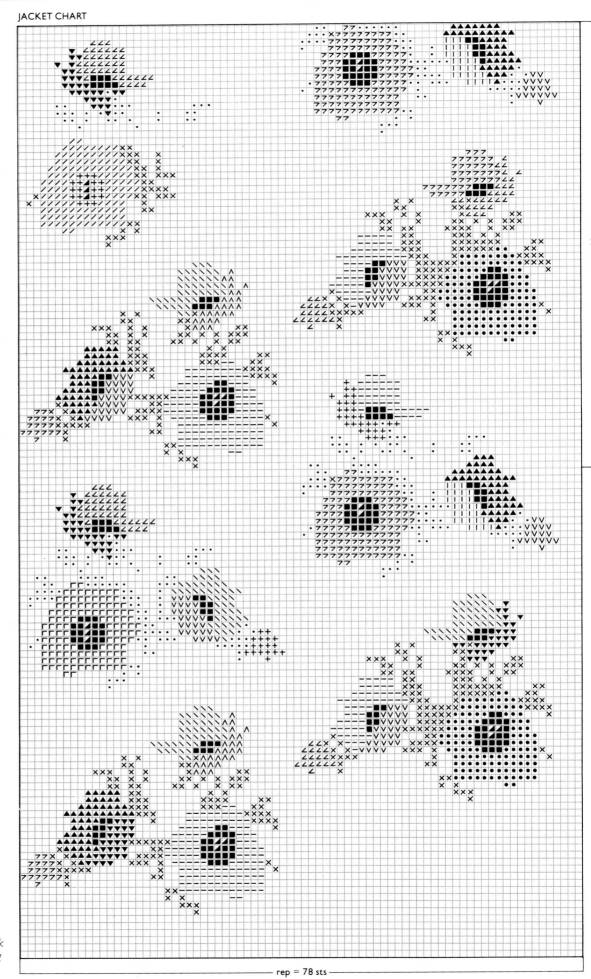

rep = 64 rows

rep = 78 sts

(Right) The Anemones jacket: crisp cotton yarns in bright colours on a black cardigan with a contrasting collar and cuffs in claret.

Change to 3mm (US2) needles and yarn A and work in rib and st st colour patt from chart, working the background colour (A) in K1, P4 rib instead of st st throughout.
1st row (rs) P4, (K1, P4) to end.
2nd row K4, (P1, K4) to end.
Rep these 2 rows twice more, inc 1 st at each end of next row. 101 sts.
7th row Rib 12, work 7th row of chart, keeping sections in yarn A in K1, P4 rib as set and motifs in st st, rib 11.
8th row Rib 11, work 8th row of chart keeping rib and motifs correct, rib 12.
Cont in this way working motifs with rib background, working 9th-134th chart rows, then rep 71st-134th rows to form patt, *at the same time* inc and work into K1, P4 rib 1 st at each end of next and every foll 6th row until there are 115 sts.
Cont straight until work measures 43cm (17in) from cast-on edge, ending with a ws row.
Shape top
Cast off 7 sts at beg of next 2 rows and 4 sts at beg of foll 4 rows. Dec 1 st at each end of next and every foll alt row until 75 sts rem, then at each end of every row until 67 sts rem. Dec 1 st at each end of every foll 3rd row until 41 sts rem.
Cast off 10 sts at beg of next 2 rows. 21 sts. Cast off.

RIGHT FRONT
Using 2¾mm (US2) needles and yarn A, cast on 88 sts. Work 16 rows in K1, P1 rib.
Change to 3mm (US2) needles and work in colour patt from chart.
1st row (rs) K 1st row of chart, (P4A, K1A) twice.
2nd row (ws) (P1A, K4A) twice, P 2nd row of chart.
These 2 rows establish the position of chart with edge sts in rib. Work 134 rows of chart then rep 71st-134th rows to form patt until right front matches back to armhole, ending at side edge.
Shape armhole and front neck
Next row Cast off 7 sts, patt to last 2 sts, work 2 tog.
Next row Work to end.
Next row Cast off 7 sts, patt to end.
Dec 1 st at armhole edge on next and 6 foll alt rows, *at the same time* dec 1 st at neck edge on next and every foll 3rd row until 45 sts rem.
Now work straight until right front matches back to shoulder, ending at armhole edge.
Shape shoulder
Cast off 15 sts at beg of next and foll alt row.
Work 1 row.
Cast off rem 15 sts.

LEFT FRONT
Using 2¾mm (US2) needles and yarn A, cast on 88 sts. Work 16 rows in K1, P1 rib.
Change to 3mm (US2) needles and work in colour patt from chart.
1st row (rs) (P4A, K1A) twice, work 1st row of chart.
2nd row (ws) Work 2nd row of chart, (P1A, K4A) twice.
These 2 rows establish the position of chart with edge sts in rib.
Now complete as given for right front, reversing all shapings.

SLEEVES
Using 2¾mm (US2) needles and yarn L, cast on 66 sts. Work 10cm (4in) in K1, P1 rib, ending with a rs row.
Inc row (ws) (Rib twice into next st, rib 1) to end. 99 sts.

FRONT BANDS AND COLLAR
Join shoulder seams.
Using 3mm (US2) needles and yarn A, cast on 10 sts. Work in K1, P1 rib until left front band, when slightly stretched, fits up to beg of front neck shaping, ending at inner front edge.
Shape collar
Change to yarn L. Now work in moss st, inc 1 st at end of next and every foll alt row until there are 22 sts. Mark corresponding position of length of band on right front with a coloured thread.
Work straight until collar fits to coloured marker, ending at inner neck edge.
Cont in moss st, dec 1 st at end of next and every alt row until 10 sts rem. Change to yarn A.
Place 7 button markers on left front band, one 1cm (½in) from cast-on edge and one at beg of collar shaping, and the rest spaced evenly between.
Work right front band.
Cont in K1, P1 rib, making buttonholes to correspond with button markers on left front band as foll:
1st buttonhole row (rs) Rib 4, cast off 2 sts, rib to end.
2nd buttonhole row Rib to end, casting on 2 sts over those cast off in previous row.
Cont in this way until band is long enough to fit right front edge. Cast off in rib.

TO MAKE UP
Join on collar and front bands, matching centre of collar to centre back neck and stretching front bands slightly to fit between cast-on edges of fronts and beg of front neck shaping.
Fold collar on to rs.
Collar edging
With rs of collar facing, using 3mm (US2) circular needle and yarn L, K up 24 sts evenly along shaped edge of collar, 1 st from lapel point (mark this st), 178 sts along straight edge of collar, 1 st from lapel point (mark this st), then 24 sts evenly along shaped edge of collar. 228 sts. Work in rows.
Work 4 rows in K1, P1 rib, inc 1 st at each side of marked sts on every row. Cast off in rib.
Set in sleeves easing any fullness over the shoulder section. Join side and sleeve seams.
Sew on buttons.

(Opposite) The black colourway of Red Roses (left, page 24) and a full back view of the black wool Anemones cardigan.

Red Roses

This, for me, is a relatively simple design – only 12 colours are used in this scattering of sprigs of red roses on a quite plain background. A string of multi-coloured embossed leaves edges the neck.

SIZE
To fit one size only up to 97cm (38in) bust
Actual width measurement 105cm (41¼in)
Length to shoulder 60cm (23½in)
Sleeve seam 53.5cm (21in)

MATERIALS
450g (18oz) 4-ply in main colour (A)
50g (2oz) in each of 4 contrast colours
   (B, F, J, M)
25g (1oz) in each of 7 contrast colours
   (C, D, E, G, H, L, N)
1 pair each 3mm (US2) and 3¼mm (US3) needles
2 3mm (US2) circular needles

TENSION
32 sts and 36 rows to 10cm (4in) over chart patt
on 3¼mm (US3) needles.

BACK
Using 3mm (US2) needles and yarn A, cast on 167
sts.
Cont in K2, P3 rib:
1st row (rs) K2, (P3, K2) to end.
2nd row P2, (K3, P2) to end.
Rep last 2 rows for 5cm (2in), ending with a 2nd
row, inc 1 st at end of last row. 168 sts.
Change to 3¼mm (US3) needles and beg colour
patt from chart on part 26 working in st st
throughout; use separate lengths of yarn for each
colour area, twisting yarns tog at colour joins to
avoid holes.
1st row (rs) K19A, (work 1st row of chart) twice,
K19A.
2nd row P19A, (work 2nd row of chart) twice,
P19A.
These 2 rows establish the position of the chart
with edge sts in st st and yarn A.
Cont in this way until 80 rows of chart have been
completed, then work 15th–48th rows again, ending
with a P row.
Shape armholes
Keeping chart correct, cast off 5 sts at beg of next
2 rows.
Dec 1 st at each end of next and every foll alt row
until 148 sts rem. **
Now cont straight until 80th row of chart has been
completed, then work 15th–60th rows again *but*
only complete the rose motif already started, do
not work second rose motif.
Cont in st st and yarn A only. Work 6 rows, ending
with a P row.
Shape shoulders
Cast off 14 sts at beg of next 4 rows and 13 sts at
beg of foll 2 rows.
Cast off rem 66 sts.

*The bark background colour of the sweater almost
camouflaged against a fallen beech. I do like the contrast
of the bright reds with the muted tones.*

work in st st throughout

- □ = A
- ⊞ = B
- ⊟ = C
- ◨ = D
- ⊠ = E
- ◩ = F
- ◿ = G
- ◺ = H
- ⊡ = J
- ◹ = L
- ☑ = M
- ■ = N

80

15

— rep = 65 sts —

FRONT
Work as given for back to **.
Now cont straight until 80th row of chart has been completed, then work 15th-56th rows again *but* only complete the rose motif already started, do not work second rose motif, end with a ws row.
Divide for neck
Next row Patt 59 sts and turn, leaving rem sts on a spare needle.
Next row Sl 1, P2 tog, psso, patt to end.
Next row Patt to last 3 sts, K3 tog.
Rep last 2 rows until 41 sts rem, ending at armhole edge.
Shape shoulder
Cast off 14 sts at beg of next and foll alt row.
Work 1 row.
Cast off rem 13 sts.
With rs of work facing return to sts on spare needle, rejoin yarn and cast off centre 30 sts, patt to end. 59 sts.

Next row Patt to last 3 sts, P3 tog tbl.
Next row Sl 1, K2 tog, psso, patt to end.
Rep last 2 rows until 41 sts rem. Work 1 row straight, ending at armhole edge.
Shape shoulder
Work as given for first side.

SLEEVES

Using 3mm (US2) needles and yarn A, cast on 65 sts.
Work in K2, P3 rib for 13cm (5in), ending with a 2nd row.
Change to 3¼mm (US3) needles. Cont in st st and colour patt from chart, work 1st-80th rows, then 15th-80th rows again, but do not work final part leaf motif, *at the same time* inc and work into st st and yarn A, 1 st at each end of next and every foll 3rd row until there are 143 sts.
Shape sleeve top
Now cont in st st in yarn A only, cast off 5 sts at beg of next 2 rows. Dec 1 st at each end of next and every foll alt row until 123 sts rem, ending with a P row.
Cast off.

NECK EDGING

Using 3mm (US2) needles and yarn A, cast on 8 sts.
1st row (rs) K5A, using yarn F, yfwd, K1, yfwd, K2.
2nd row P6F, using yarn A, K into front and back of next st, K3.
3rd row K4A, P1A, using yarn F, K2, yfwd, K1, yfwd, K3.
4th row P8F, using yarn A, K into front and back of next st, K4.
5th row K4A, P2A, using yarn F, K3, yfwd, K1, yfwd, K4.
6th row P10F, using yarn A, K into front and back of next st, K5.
7th row K4A, P3A, using yarn F, K4, yfwd, K1, yfwd, K5.
8th row P12F, using yarn A, K into front and back of next st, K6.
9th row K4A, P4A, using yarn F, sl 1, K1, psso, K7, K2 tog, K1.
10th row P10F, using yarn A, K into front and back of next st, K7.
11th row K4A, P5A, using yarn F, sl 1, K1, psso, K5, K2 tog, K1.

12th row P8F, using yarn A, K into front and back of next st, K2A, P1E, K5A.
13th row K4A, P1A, K1E, P4A, using yarn F, sl 1, K1, psso, K3, K2 tog, K1.
14th row P6F, using yarn A, K into front and back of next st, K3A, P1E, K5A.
15th row K4A, P1A, K1E, P5A, using yarn F, sl 1, K1, psso, K1, K2 tog, K1.
16th row P4F, using yarn A, K into front and back of next st, K4A, P1E, K5A.
17th row K4A, P1A, K1E, P6A, using yarn F, sl 1, K2 tog, psso, K1.
18th row P2F tog, using yarn A, cast off 5 sts, (1 st rem on right-hand needle), P1A, P1E, P1A, K4A. 8 sts.
Work another 10 leaves in colour sequence (E, E, F, B, E) twice, as foll:
Rep 1st-18th rows but using E instead of F.
*** Rep 1st-18th rows but using E instead of F and F instead of E. ·
Rep 1st-18th rows but using B instead of E.
Rep 1st-18th rows but using B instead of F.
Rep 1st-18th rows but using E instead of F. ***
Rep from *** to *** again.
Rep 1st-18th rows but using E instead of F and A instead of E.
Cast off rem 8 sts.
With rs of work facing, using first 3mm (US2) circular needle and yarn A, K up 148 sts evenly along straight edge of edging.
Cut yarn and leave sts on needle.

NECKBAND

Join right shoulder seam. With rs of work facing, using second 3mm (US2) circular needle and yarn A, K up 19 sts down left side of neck, 34 sts across front neck, 19 sts up right side of neck and 76 sts across back neck. 148 sts. Work in rows.
Work 5 rows K1, P1 rib.
Join in edging
Next row (rs) (Holding needle with sts of edging with rs facing in front of neckband sts, rib tog 1 st from each needle to join work) to end.
Rib 2 rows.
Cast off in rib.

TO MAKE UP

Join left shoulder seam and neckband seam.
Set in sleeves. Join side and sleeve seams.

The embossed leaf edging lifts the evenness of the stocking stitch sweater.

Hollyhocks

So many flowers can look alike when simplified and stylized for knitting, but these wide open flower heads are unmistakably hollyhocks. I particularly like the way the flower grows out of the ribbed welt (below).

SIZE
To fit one size only up to 91cm (36in) bust
Actual width measurement 98cm (38½in)
Length to shoulder 65cm (25½in)
Sleeve seam 48cm (18¾in)

MATERIALS
400g (16oz) 4-ply in main colour (A)
50g (2oz) in 1 contrast colour (C)
25g (1oz) in each of 14 contrast colours
 (B, D, E, F, G, H, J, L, M, N, Q, R, S, T)
1 pair each 2¾mm (US2) and 3mm (US2) needles
2.50mm (USC) crochet hook

TENSION
29 sts and 39 rows to 10cm (4in) over chart patt on 3mm (US2) needles. ·

BACK
Using 2¾mm (US2) needles and yarn A, cast on 143 sts. Work in K3, P2 rib.
1st row (rs) K3, (P2, K3) to end.
2nd row P3, (K2, P3) to end.
Rep last 2 rows 7 times more.
Change to 3mm (US2) needles and beg colour patt from chart, working in st st unless otherwise indicated. Keep rib sections correct for 1st-26th rows and use separate lengths of yarn for each colour area, twisting yarns tog at colour joins to avoid holes. Work 1st-100th rows, then rep 31st-100th rows until work measures 41cm (16in) from cast-on edge, ending with a P row.

I like to use moss stitch for these Peter Pan collars because it sits so well.

Shape armholes
Cast off 8 sts at beg of next 2 rows. 127 sts. **
Now cont straight until work measures 24cm (9½in) from beg of armhole shaping, ending with a P row.
Shape shoulders
Cast off 14 sts at beg of next 6 rows.
Cast off rem 43 sts.

FRONT
Work as given for back to **.
Now cont straight until work measures 19cm (7½in) from beg of armhole shaping, ending with a P row.
Divide for neck
Next row Patt 46 sts and turn, leaving rem sts on a spare needle.
Dec 1 st at neck edge on next and every foll alt row until 42 sts rem.
Now work straight until front matches back to shoulder, ending with a P row.
Shape shoulder
Cast off 14 sts at beg of next and foll alt row.
Work 1 row. Cast off rem 14 sts.
With rs of work facing return to sts on spare needle, rejoin yarn and cast off centre 35 sts, patt to end. 46 sts.
Complete as given for first side.

SLEEVES
Using 2¾mm (US2) needles and yarn A, cast on 63 sts. Work 26 rows in K3, P2 rib as given for back.
K 4 rows.

This deep welted cotton design has the delicate feeling of a certain type of 18th-century French wallpaper – it's to do with the combination of vertical patterns worked in powdery colours.

rep = 70 rows

work in st st throughout unless otherwise indicated

sleeves = 93 sts
back = 143 sts

☐ = using A, K on rs rows, P on ws rows   ☑ = using A, P on rs rows, K on ws rows

☐ = using A, K on rs rows, P on ws rows

B =
C =
D =
E =
F =
G =
H =
J =
L =
M =
N =
Q =
R =
S =

Inc row K1, (K1, K twice into next st) to last 2 sts, K2. 93 sts. K 1 row.
Change to 3mm (US2) needles and beg colour patt from chart as given for back. Work 26 rows, inc and work into rib 1 st at each end of next and every foll 4th row. 107 sts.
Next row Moss st 7, work 27th row from chart over next 93 sts, moss st 7.
Now cont in this way, working centre 93 sts from chart, but inc and work into moss st 1 st at each

end of 2nd and every foll 4th row until there are 139 sts.
Cont straight until work measures 48cm (18¾in) from cast-on edge, ending with a P row.
Cast off.

COLLAR
Using 2¾mm (US2) needles and yarn A, cast on 105 sts. Work 8cm (3in) in moss st.
Cast off in patt.

TO MAKE UP
Join shoulder seams. Sew cast-on edge of collar around neck edge, beg and ending at centre front neck.
Collar edging
Using 2.50mm (USC) crochet hook and yarn A, work crochet picot edging as foll:
1st row Work in double crochet around collar edge.
2nd row * 1 double crochet into each of next 3 double crochet, 4 chain, slip st into last double crochet; rep from *.
Set in sleeves, sewing cast-off edge around entire armhole. Join side and sleeve seams.

Strangely, the hollyhocks appear larger when worked on black, which gives quite a different look to the cream version.

Floral
Geometrics

Indian Weave

In once admired a beautiful woven Guatemalan purse that someone was carrying around at an exhibition, and was delighted when she simply emptied it of its contents and gave it to me. I particularly liked the way the flowers seemed simply strewn on to a patterned background and used the idea in a waistcoat and cardigan. It's extraordinary how varying the colours from the soft candies of the cardigan to the rich glowing tones of the waistcoat can make a basically similar design look so very different.

CARDIGAN

SIZE
To fit one size only up to 96cm (38in) bust
Actual width measurement 102cm (40in)
Length to shoulder 65cm (25½in)
Sleeve seam 50cm (19½in)

MATERIALS
250g (10oz) 4-ply in main colour (A)
100g (4oz) in each of 4 contrast colours
   (B, C, L, N)
50g(2oz) in 1 contrast colour (E)
25g (1oz) in each of 11 contrast colours
   (D, F, G, H, J, M, Q, R, S, T, U)
1 pair each 2¾mm (US1) and 3¼mm (US3) needles
2.50mm (USC) crochet hook
11 buttons

TENSION
30 sts and 34 rows to 10cm (4in) over chart patt
on 3¼mm (US3) needles.

BACK
Using 2¾mm (US1) needles and yarn A, cast on
150 sts.
Work 16 rows in K1 tbl, P1 rib.
Change to 3¼mm (US3) needles and commence
main patt. ** Work 2 rows st st.
Next row (K1A, 1B) 4 times, 5A, *(1A, 1B) 18
times, 5A, rep from * twice more, (1A, 1B) 7 times.
Next row (P1B, 1A) 7 times, *5A, (1B, 1A) 18
times, rep from * twice more, 5A, (1B, 1A) 4 times.
Now cont in st st and commence colour patt from
chart 1, working in st st throughout; use separate
lengths of yarn for each colour area and twist yarns
tog at colour joins to avoid holes, work 1st-11th
rows.
Next row (P1H, 1A) 7 times, *5A, (1H, 1A) 18
times, rep from * twice more, 5A, (1H, 1A) 4
times.
Next row (K1A, 1H) 4 times, 5A, *(1A, 1H) 18
times, 5A, rep from * twice more, (1A, 1H) 7
times.

The softly coloured, candy, cotton cardigan against a dramatic bed of tall reeds. I can also see this on a beach in Mexico.

Cont in yarn A, work 3 rows st st, ending with a P row.
Cont in st st and colour patt from chart 2.
Next row K6A, (work 1st row of chart 2) twice, K6A.
Next row P6A, (work 2nd row of chart 2) twice, P6A.
These 2 rows set the position of chart 2 with st st edge sts. Work a further 58 rows.
The last 80 rows form the main patt. Keeping patt correct, beg at ** work a further 50 rows, ending with a ws row.

Shape armholes
Cast off 7 sts at beg of next 2 rows. 136 sts.
Now work 66 rows straight ending with a ws row and only completing the final whole motifs.
Now cont in yarn A only. Work 10 rows.
Cast off.

RIGHT FRONT
Using 2¾mm (US1) needles and yarn A, cast on 74 sts. Work 16 rows in K1 tbl, P1 rib, inc 1 st at side edge of last row. 75 sts.
Change to 3¼mm (US3) needles and commence main patt. Work 2 rows st st.

Next row K1A, (1B, 1A) 18 times, 5A, (1B, 1A) 16 times, 1B.
Next row P1B, (1A, 1B) 16 times, 5A, (1A, 1B) 18 times, 1A.
Now commence colour patt from chart 1. Work 1st-11th rows.
Next row P1H, (1A, 1H) 16 times, 5A, (1A, 1H) 18 times, 1A.
Next row K1A, (1H, 1A) 18 times, 5A, (1H, 1A) 16 times, 1H.
Cont in yarn A, work 3 rows st st, ending with a P row.
Now work 60 rows of chart 2, working between front markers. These 80 rows form the main patt.
Cont in patt until right front matches back to armhole, ending at side edge.

Shape armhole
Cast off 7 sts at beg of next row. 68 sts.
Keeping patt correct as given for back, work a further 58 rows straight, ending at front edge.

Shape neck
Cast off 12 sts at beg of next row, then cast off 2 sts at beg of every foll alt row until 40 sts rem, ending with a ws row.
Cast off.

CARDIGAN CHART 1

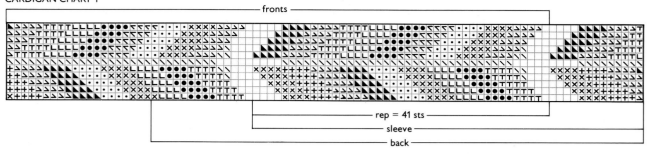

CARDIGAN CHART 2

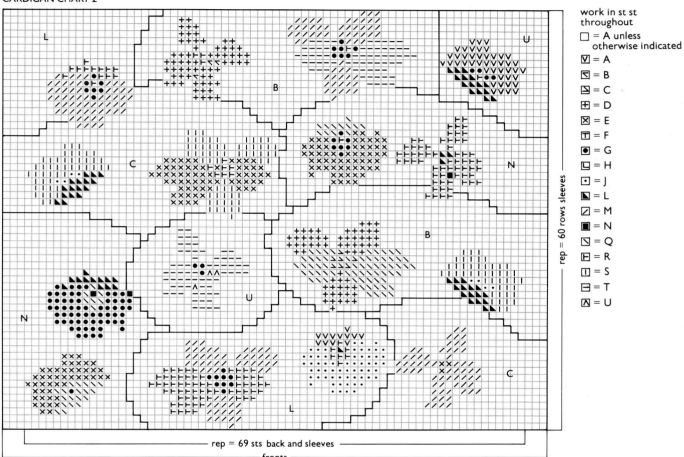

work in st st
throughout

☐ = A unless
    otherwise indicated
Ⓥ = A
◪ = B
◪ = C
⊞ = D
⊠ = E
⊤ = F
⊙ = G
Ⅼ = H
· = J
◼ = L
◺ = M
◼ = N
◹ = Q
⊞ = R
Ⅱ = S
⊟ = T
◮ = U

rep = 60 rows sleeves

rep = 69 sts back and sleeves
fronts

LEFT FRONT
Work as given for right front, making a mirror image of chart I by reading rs rows from left to right and ws rows from right to left and reversing shapings.

SLEEVES
Using 2¾mm (US1) needles and yarn A, cast on 64 sts. Work in K1 tbl, P1 rib for 13cm (5in), ending with a rs row.
Inc row Rib 2, (inc in next st, rib 1) 31 times. 95 sts.
Change to 3¼mm (US3) needles and work 2 rows st st.
Next row (K1A, 1B) 4 times, 5A, *(1A, 1B) 18 times, 5A, rep from * again.
Next row *P5A, (1B, 1A) 18 times, rep from * again, 5A, (1B, 1A) 4 times.
Now commence colour patt from chart I. Work 1st-11th rows.
Next row *P5A, (1H, 1A) 18 times, rep from * again, 5A, (1H, 1A) 4 times.
Next row (K1A, 1H) 4 times, 5A, *(1A, 1H) 18 times, 5A, rep from * again.
Cont in yarn A, work 3 rows st st, ending with a P

A collar detail from the Indian Weave cardigan.

row. Cont in colour patt from chart 2 as foll:
Next row K13A, work 1st row of chart 2, K13A.
Next row P13A, work 2nd row of chart 2, P13A.
These 2 rows set the chart with st st edge sts.
Cont as set, inc and work into st st and yarn A, 1 st
at each end of next and every foll 3rd row until
there are 139 sts. Cont straight until work
measures 50cm (19½in) from cast-on edge, ending
with a ws row. Cast off.

BUTTON BAND
Join shoulder seams. Using 2¾mm (US1) needles
and yarn A, cast on 11 sts.
1st row (rs) K1 tbl, (P1, K1 tbl) to end.
2nd row P1, (K1 tbl, P1) to end.
Rep last 2 rows until left front band, when slightly
stretched, fits up to beg of front neck shaping,
ending at inner front edge.
Cut yarn and leave sts on a holder.
Place 11 button markers on left front band, one
1cm (½in) from cast-on and one 1cm (½in) below
neck, and the rest spaced evenly between.

BUTTONHOLE BAND
Work as given for button band but end at outer
edge and do not cut yarn, making buttonholes
opposite markers on left front band as foll:
1st buttonhole row (rs) Rib 4, cast off 3, rib to end.
2nd buttonhole row Rib to end, casting on 3 sts
over those cast off in previous row.

COLLAR
With rs of work facing, using 2¾mm (US1) needles
and yarn A, rib across 11 sts of buttonhole band, K
up 31 sts up right front neck, 45 sts across back
neck and 31 sts down left front neck, rib across 11
sts of button band. 129 sts. Cont in K1 tbl, P1 rib
for 8cm (3in). Cast off loosely in rib.

TO MAKE UP
Join on front bands.
Collar edging
Using 2.50mm (USC) crochet hook and yarn A,
work crochet picot edging as foll:
1st row Work in double crochet around collar
edge.
2nd row *1 double crochet into each of next 3
double crochet, 4 chain, slip st into last double
crochet; rep from *.
Sew cast-off edge of sleeves around entire armhole
edge. Join side and sleeve seams.
Sew on buttons.

Theatrical lighting cast from stormy winter skies throws out the colour of the burgundy wool waistcoat version of the Indian Weave design.

WAISTCOAT

SIZE
To fit one size only up to 91cm (36in) bust
Actual width measurement 97cm (38¼in)
Length to shoulder 63.5cm (25in)

MATERIALS
150g (6oz) 4-ply in main colour (A)
50g (2oz) in each of 3 contrast colours (H, N, Q)
25g (1oz) in each of 12 contrast colours
   (B, C, D, E, F, G, J, L, M, R, S, T)
1 pair each 3mm (US2) and 3¼mm (US3) needles
3mm (US2) circular needle
Cable needle
10 buttons

TENSION
30 sts and 36 rows to 10cm (4in) over chart patt
on 3¼mm (US3) needles.

SPECIAL ABBREVIATIONS
C4F (cable 4 front) – sl next 2 sts on to cable
needle and hold at front, K2, then K2 from cable
needle.

BACK
Using 3mm (US2) needles and yarn A, cast on 142
sts. Work 10 rows in K1 tbl, P1 rib.
Change to 3¼mm (US3) needles and beg cable rib
patt:
1st row (rs) K1, *P4, K4; rep from * to last 5 sts,
P4, K1.
2nd row P1, *K4, P4; rep from * to last 5 sts, K4,
P1.
3rd-4th rows Rep 1st-2nd rows.
5th row K1, *P4, C4F, P4, K4; rep from * to last 13
sts, P4, C4F, P4, K1.
6th row As 2nd row.
These 6 rows form the cable rib patt.
Rep them 4 times more, inc 1 st at centre of last
row. 143 sts.
Beg with a K row, work 2 rows st st.
Commence colour patt from chart 1 on page 40
working in st st throughout; use separate lengths of
yarn for each colour area and twist yarns tog at
colour joins to avoid holes.
Next row K25A, work 1st row of chart 1 between
back markers, K25A.
Next row P25A,, work 2nd row of chart 1
between back markers, P25A.
These 2 rows set the chart with st st edge sts.

WAISTCOAT CHART 1

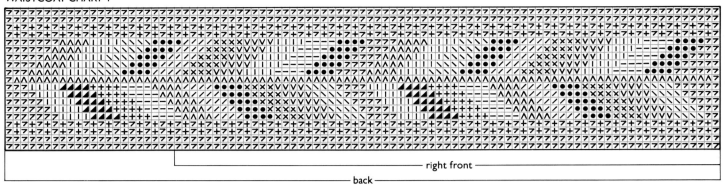

right front ——
back ——

work in st st only

$\boxed{7}$ = B

$\boxplus$ = C

$\boxed{\searrow}$ = D

$\boxed{V}$ = E

$\boxtimes$ = F

$\boxed{\bullet}$ = G

$\boxed{/}$ = H

$\boxed{\wedge}$ = J

$\boxminus$ = L

$\blacksquare$ = M

$\boxed{|}$ = N

$\boxed{\cdot}$ = Q

$\blacksquare$ = R

$\boxed{7}$ = S

$\boxed{\searrow}$ = T

WAISTCOAT CHART 2

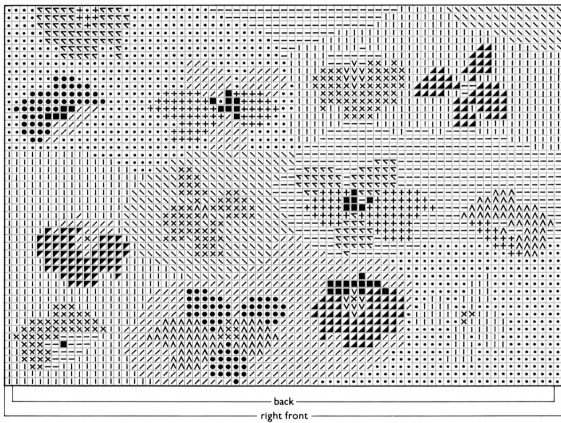

back ——
right front ——

Keeping chart correct, work a further 17 rows.
Cont in st st.
Next row With yarn A, P to end.
Next row K37A, work 1st row of chart 2 between
back markers, K37A.
Next row P37A, work 2nd row of chart 2
between back markers, P37A.
These 2 rows set the chart with st st edge sts.
Keeping chart correct, work a further 48 rows.
The last 70 rows form the colour patt. Keeping
patt correct cont until work measures 44.5cm
(17½in) from cast-on edge, ending with a ws row.
Shape armholes
Cast off 7 sts at beg of next 2 rows. Now dec 1 st
each end next and every foll alt row until 123 sts
rem.
Now work straight until back measures 19cm
(7½in) from beg of armhole shaping, ending with a
ws row.
Shape shoulders
Cast off 13 sts at beg of next 2 rows and 14 sts at
beg of next 4 rows. 41 sts.
Cast off.

RIGHT FRONT

Using 3mm (US2) needles and yarn A, cast on 70 sts.
Work 10 rows in K1 tbl, P1 rib.
Change to 3¼mm (US3) needles and work in cable and rib patt:
1st row (rs) K5, *P4, K4; rep from * to last st, K1.
2nd row P5, *K4, P4; rep from * to last st, P1.
3rd-4th rows As 1st-2nd rows.
5th row K5, *P4, C4F, P4, K4; rep from * to last st, K1.
6th row As 2nd row.
These 6 rows form the cable and rib patt. Rep them 4 times more, inc 1 st at centre of last row. 71 sts.
Beg with a K row, work 2 rows st st.
Commence colour patt:
Work 19 rows of chart 1, working between right front markers.
Next row With yarn A, P to end.
Work 50 rows of chart 2, working between right front markers.
These 70 rows form the colour patt. Cont in patt until right front matches back to armhole, ending at side edge.

Shape armhole and front neck
Next row Cast off 7 sts, work in patt to last 2 sts, P2 tog.
Keeping patt correct, dec 1 st at armhole edge on next and 7 foll alt rows, *at the same time* dec 1 st at neck edge on every foll 4th row until 41 sts rem.
Now work straight until right front matches back to shoulder, ending at armhole edge.

Shape shoulder
Cast off 13 sts at beg of next row and 14 sts at beg of foll alt row.
Work 1 row.
Cast off rem 14 sts.

LEFT FRONT

Work as given above for right front, reversing all shapings.

FRONT BANDS AND COLLAR

Join shoulder seams.
Using 3mm (US2) needles and yarn A, cast on 10 sts.

Work left front band
Work in K1 tbl, P1 rib until left front band, when slightly stretched, fits up to beg of front neck shaping, ending at inner front edge.

Shape collar
Now work in moss st, *at the same time* inc 1 st at end of next and every foll alt row until there are 22 sts.
Mark corresponding position of length of band on right front with a coloured thread.
Work straight until collar fits to coloured marker, ending at inner neck edge.
Cont in moss st, dec 1 st at end of next and every alt row until 10 sts rem.
Place 10 button markers on left front band, one 1cm (½in) from cast-on edge and one at beg of collar shaping, and the remaining markers spaced evenly between.

Work right front band
Cont in K1 tbl, P1 rib, making buttonholes to correspond with button markers on left front band as foll:
1st buttonhole row (rs) Rib 4, cast off 2 sts, rib to end.
2nd buttonhole row Rib to end, casting on 2 sts over those cast off in previous row.
Cont in this way until right front band matches left front band to cast-on edge. Cast off in rib.

ARMBANDS

With rs of work facing, using 3mm (US2) circular needle and yarn A, K up 138 sts evenly around armhole edge.
Work in rows.
Work 6 rows in K1 tbl, P1 rib.
Cast off in rib.

TO MAKE UP

Join on collar and front bands, matching centre of collar to centre back neck and stretching front bands slightly to fit between cast-on edges of fronts and beg of front neck shaping.
Fold collar on to rs.

Collar edging
With rs of collar facing, using 3mm (US2) circular needle and yarn A, K up 197 sts evenly around edge of collar.
Work in rows.
Work 6 rows in K1 tbl, P1 rib.
Cast off in rib.
Join side seams.
Sew on buttons.

Tartan Flower

The pattern and colouring of a Buchanan tartan is the background to large stylized flowers. It's interesting how the fresh clean flat colour of the flowers makes them appear to float above the 'woven' fabric. The jacket has a shawl collar, and the waistcoat, which can be worn by men or women, is similarly long and loose.

JACKET

SIZE
To fit one size only up to 101cm (40in) bust
Actual width measurement 125cm (49¼in)
Length to shoulder 73cm (28¾in)
Sleeve seam 48cm (18¾in)

MATERIALS
250g (10oz) 4-ply in main colour (A)
175g (7oz) in 1 contrast colour (E)
150g (6oz) in 1 contrast colour (B)
75g (3oz) in 1 contrast colour (C)
50g (2oz) in each of 3 contrast colours (D, J, L)
25g (1oz) in each of 6 contrast colours
   (F, G, H, M, N, Q)
1 pair each 3mm (US2) and 3¼mm (US3) needles
3mm (US2) circular needle
8 buttons

TENSION
29 sts and 31 rows to 10cm (4in) over chart patt on 3¼mm (US3) needles

BACK
Using 3mm (US2) needles and yarn A, cast on 173 sts.
Work in two-colour rib, keep yarn not in use on ws of work, stranding loosely:
1st row (rs) *K1A, K1C, K1A, P2A; rep from * to last 3 sts, K1A, K1B, K1A.
2nd row *P1A, P1C, P1A, K2A; rep from * to last 3 sts, P1A, P1C, P1A.
These 2 rows form the two-colour rib.
Cont until work measures 5cm (2in) from cast-on edge, ending with a ws row, inc 2 sts evenly across last row. 175 sts.
Change to 3¼mm (US3) needles and commence colour patt from chart 1 on page 44, working in st st throughout; use separate lengths of yarn for each colour area, twisting yarns tog at colour joins to avoid holes.
1st row (rs) K13A, (work 60 sts from X to Z) twice, work 29 sts from X to Y, K13A.
2nd row P13A, work 29 sts from Y to X, (work 60 sts from Z to X) twice, P13A.
These 2 rows establish edge sts in yarn A and st st and position of chart 1.
Cont as set until 138 rows have been worked from chart, ending with a P row.
Shape armholes
Keeping chart correct, cast off 8 sts at beg of next 2 rows.
Dec 1 st at each end of every foll alt row until 149 sts rem.
Now cont straight until 210 rows have been worked from chart, ending with a P row.
Shape shoulders
Cast off 17 sts at beg of next 2 rows and 18 sts at beg of foll 4 rows.
Cast off rem 43 sts.

POCKET LININGS (make 2)
Using 3¼mm (US3) needles and yarn A, cast on 35 sts.
Beg with a K row, work 48 rows st st.
Cut yarn and leave sts on a spare needle.

LEFT FRONT
Using 3mm (US2) needles and yarn A, cast on 88 sts.
Work 5cm (2in) in two-colour rib as given for back, ending with a ws row, inc 1 st at side edge of last row. 89 sts.
Change to 3¼mm (US3) needles. Commence colour patt from chart 1:
1st row (rs) Work 60 sts from X to Z, then work 29 sts from X to Y.
2nd row Work 29 sts from Y to X, then work 60 sts from Z to X.
These 2 rows establish the patt. Cont as set until 62 rows have been worked from chart 1, ending with a P row.
Place pocket
Next row Patt 27 sts, sl next 35 sts on to a holder, patt across 35 sts of first pocket lining, patt 27 sts.
Now cont working from chart until work measures same as back to armhole, ending at side edge.
Shape armhole and neck
Next row Cast off 8 sts, patt to last 2 sts, work 2 tog. **
Work 1 row.
*** Dec 1 st at armhole edge on next and 4 foll alt rows, *at the same time* dec 1 st at neck edge on 3rd row from previous dec, then on every foll 2nd and 3rd row alternately until 53 sts rem.
Now cont straight until work measures same as back to shoulder shaping, ending at armhole edge.
Shape shoulder
Cast off 17 sts at beg of next row and 18 sts at beg of foll alt row.
Work 1 row.
Cast off rem 18 sts.

RIGHT FRONT
Work as given for left front to **.
Now complete as given for left front from *** to end.

SLEEVES
Using 3mm (US2) needles and yarn A, cast on 63 sts.
Work in K1, P1 rib as foll:
1st row (rs) K1, (P1, K1) to end.
2nd row P1, (K1, P1) to end.
Rep last 2 rows for 5cm (2in), ending with a ws row.
Now work a further 10cm (4in) in two-colour rib as given for back, ending with a rs row.
Inc row Rib 6, (inc in next st, rib 1) 25 times, inc in next st, rib 6. 89 sts.

The Tartan Flower jacket and the waistcoat on page 46 both have patterned front bands which, I find, help to link the two fronts in this sort of densely patterned design.

JACKET CHART 1

□ = A
⊠ = B
◉ = C
⊘ = D
⊓ = E
◣ = F
◪ = G
■ = H
◹ = J
◩ = L
▼ = M
◮ = N
⊤ = Q

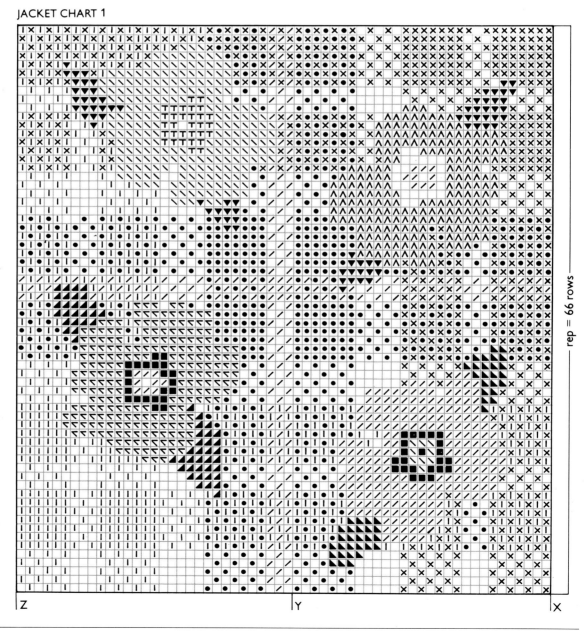

rep = 66 rows

Z   Y   X

Change to 3¼mm (US3) needles and work in colour patt from chart I as given for left front, *at the same time* inc and work into yarn A and st st I st at each end of next and every foll 4th row until there are 139 sts.
Cont straight until work measures 51cm (20in) from cast-on edge, ending with a ws row, completing only whole flower motifs. Cast off.

FRONT BAND AND COLLAR
Join shoulder seams.
Using 3mm (US2) needles and yarn A, cast on 11 sts.
Cont in rib as foll:
1st row (rs) (KI, PI) to last st, KI.
2nd row (PI, KI) to last st, PI.
1st buttonhole row Rib 4, cast off 3, rib to end.
2nd buttonhole row Rib to end, casting on 3 sts over those cast off in previous row.
Now work 40 rows in rib and st st from chart 2, making buttonholes as shown. Rep the 40 rows until 8 buttonholes in all have been made, *at the same time* working flower motifs in yarns C, L, D, Q and B.
Work 2 rows rib as set, ending with a ws row.
Shape collar
Inc I st at beg of next and every foll alt row until there are 20 sts, ending with a rs row.
Now, beg with rs of collar facing, cont to work in rib and st st from chart 3, *at the same time* inc at outer edge on every foll alt row until there are 25 sts. Mark corresponding position of length of band to this point on left front neck.
Cont straight until 53 rows have been worked from chart 3, then rep 10th–53rd rows until collar fits up right front, across back neck and down left front to coloured marker.
Dec I st at outer edge on next and every foll alt row until 20 sts rem, working complete motifs only.
Now cont in yarn A only and rib, cont to dec as before until 11 sts rem, then cont in rib until band is long enough, when slightly stretched, to fit down left front.
Cast off in rib.

JACKET CHART 3

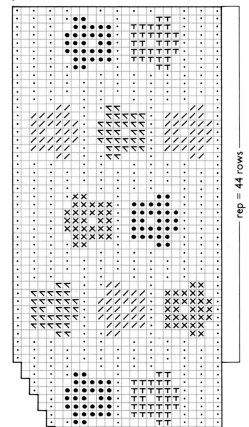

rep = 44 rows

JACKET CHART 2

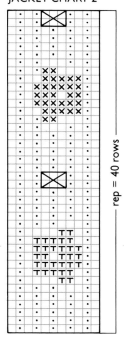

rep = 40 rows

JACKET CHART 4

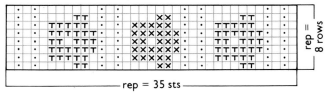

rep = 8 rows

rep = 35 sts

POCKET TOPS
With rs of work facing, using 3mm (US2) needles and yarn A, K across 35 sts of pocket top.
Beg with a 2nd row, work I row rib as given for button band.
Now work from chart 4, work 8 rows.
Cont in yarn A only, rib 2 rows.
Cast off in rib.

TO MAKE UP
Sew on front bands and collar.
Collar edging
Using 3mm (US2) circular needle and yarn A, with rs of work facing, K up 190 sts evenly around entire collar edge.
Work in rows.
Work 4 rows KI, PI rib, dec I st at each end of every row.
Cast off in rib.
Set in sleeves, sewing final rows to cast-off sts at underarm.
Join side and sleeve seams.
Sew down pocket linings and pocket tops.
Sew on buttons.

work in st st unless otherwise indicated

☐ = using A, K on rs rows, P on ws rows
⊡ = using A, P on rs rows, K on ws rows
☒ = B
⊙ = C
◪ = D
Ⅲ = E
◩ = F
◪ = G
■ = H
◨ = J
◧ = L
▼ = M
◮ = N
⊤ = Q

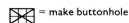 = make buttonhole

The Tartan Flower waistcoat (left) photographed with the Rowan Berries sweater (right, page 114).

WAISTCOAT

SIZES
To fit 87-91[91-97]cm (34-36[36-38]in) bust
Actual width measurement 101[107]cm
(39¾[42]in)
Length to shoulder 51[56]cm (20 [22]in)

MATERIALS
150[200]g (6[8]oz) 4-ply in main colour (A)
50g (2oz) in each of 3 contrast colours (B, C, E)
25g (1oz) in each of 8 contrast colours
   (D, F, G, H, J, L, M, N)
1 pair each 3mm (US2) and 3¼mm (US3) needles
6 buttons

TENSION
29 sts and 31 rows to 10cm (4in) over chart patt on
3¼mm (US3) needles.

BACK
Using 3mm (US2) needles and yarn A, cast on
143[151] sts.
Work in twisted rib as foll:
1st row (rs) K1 tbl, (P1, K1 tbl) to end.
2nd row P1, (K1 tbl, P1) to end.
These 2 rows form twisted rib. Work a further 6
rows.
Change to 3¼mm (US3) needles. Commence
colour patt from chart 1 on page 48 working in st
st throughout; use separate lengths of yarn for each
colour area, twisting yarns tog at colour joins to
avoid holes.
1st size only
1st row (rs) K from W to Z, X to Z, then from X
to V.
2nd row (ws) P from V to X, Z to X, then from Z
to W.
2nd size only
1st row (rs) K from U to Z, (X to Z) twice, then
from X to T.
2nd row (ws) P from T to X, (Z to X) twice, then
from Z to U.
Both sizes
These 2 rows establish the patt.
Cont as set until work measures 28[30.5]cm
(11[12]in), ending with a P row.
Shape armholes
Keeping chart correct, cast off 8[9] sts at beg of
next 2 rows.
Dec 1 st at each end of next and every foll alt row
until 121[129] sts rem. Now cont straight until work
measures 51[56]cm (20[22]in) from cast-on edge,
ending with a P row.
Shape shoulders
Cast off 11[12] sts at beg of next 4 rows and 12[14]
sts at beg of foll 2 rows. Cast off rem 53 sts.

LEFT FRONT
Using 3mm (US2) needles and yarn A, cast on 5
sts.
**Cont in twisted rib as given for back, *at the same
time* cast on and work into rib 5 sts at beg of next
and every foll alt row until there are 70[75] sts
ending with a ws row. Now work 8 rows straight
in rib as set, inc 1 st at each end of last row. 72[77]
sts.
Change to 3¼mm (US3) needles. Commence
colour patt from chart 1 working in st st
throughout.
1st row (rs) K from X to S[R].
2nd row (ws) P from S[R] to X.
These 2 rows establish the patt. Cont as set until
work measures same as back to armhole, ending at
side edge.

WAISTCOAT CHART 1

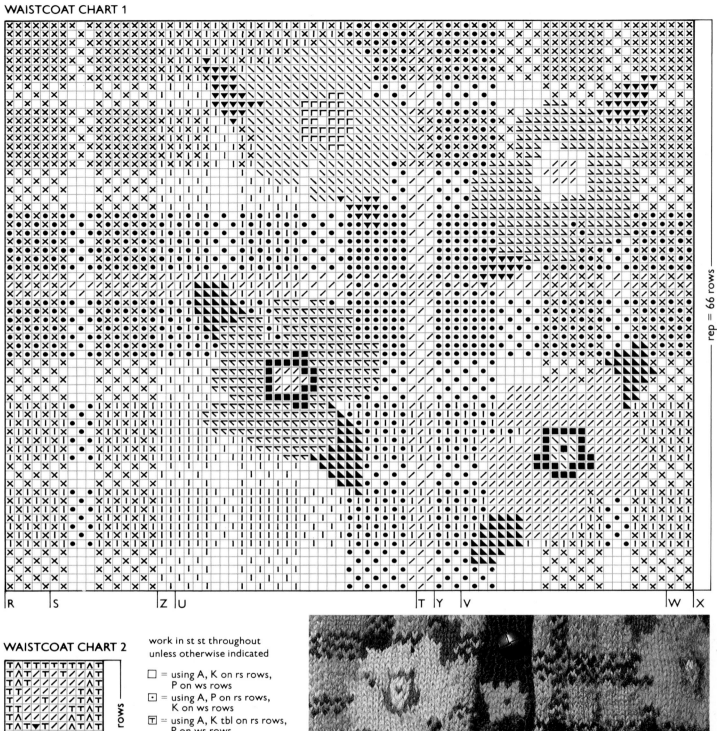

rep = 66 rows

R   S   Z U   T Y V   W X

WAISTCOAT CHART 2

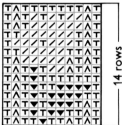

14 rows

work in st st throughout
unless otherwise indicated

☐ = using A, K on rs rows,
   P on ws rows

⊡ = using A, P on rs rows,
   K on ws rows

T̄ = using A, K tbl on rs rows,
   P on ws rows

Λ̄ = using A, P on rs rows,
   K tbl on ws rows

⊠ = B

⊙ = C

☑ = D

▥ = E

◣ = F

◼ = G

◨ = H

◪ = J

▼ = L

☐ = M

◩ = N

WAISTCOAT CHART 3

14 rows

Shape armhole and neck
Cast off 8[9] sts at beg of next row then dec I st at armhole edge on next 3[2] rows and foll 6 alt rows, *at the same time* dec I st at neck edge on next and every foll 3rd row until 34[38] sts rem. Now cont straight until work measures same as back to shoulder shaping, ending at armhole edge.
Shape shoulder
Cast off II[12] sts at beg of next row and foll alt row. Work I row.
Cast off rem 12[14] sts.

RIGHT FRONT
Using 3mm (US2) needles and yarn A, cast on 5 sts. Work I row in twisted rib as given for back. Now work as given for left front from ** to end.

ARMBANDS
Join shoulder seams.
With rs of work facing, using 3mm (US2) needles and yarn A, K up 150[166] sts. Work 6 rows KI tbl, PI rib.
Cast off evenly in rib.

FRONT BAND
Using 3mm (US2) needles and yarn A, cast on II sts.
*** Work 4 rows KI tbl, PI rib as given for back.
Ist buttonhole row (rs) Rib 4, cast off 3, rib to end of row.
2nd buttonhole row Rib to end, casting on 3 sts over those cast off.
Work 4[6] rows rib. ***
Now work 14 rows in twisted rib and st st from chart 2.
Rep from *** to *** again.
Now work 14 rows in rib and st st from chart 3.
Rep the last 48[52] rows until 6th buttonhole has been worked.
Now cont in yarn A and rib only until band is long enough, when slightly stretched, to fit up right front, across back neck and down left front.
Cast off in rib.

TO MAKE UP
Sew on front band.
Join side and armband seams. Sew on buttons.

Wavy Fair Isle

As the name suggests, instead of the rather strict horizontal bands of traditional Fair Isle, I worked these floral bands in waves flowing around the body and sleeves of the sweater and cardigan. The flower wheels are very stylized – such as you often see in art deco textiles.

CARDIGAN

SIZE
To fit one size only up to 97cm (38in) bust
Actual width measurement 103cm (40½in)
Length to shoulder 71.5cm (28¼in)
Sleeve seam 45cm (17¾in) with cuff folded back

MATERIALS
175g (7oz) 4-ply in main colour (A)
100g (4oz) in 1 contrast colour (C)
75g (3oz) in 1 contrast colour (T)
50g (2oz) in 3 contrast colours (B, J, S)
25g (1oz) in each of 12 contrast colours
  (D, E, F, G, H, L, M, N, Q, R, U, V)
1 pair each 3mm (US2) and 3¼mm (US3) needles
9 buttons

TENSION
28 sts and 35 rows to 10cm (4in) over chart patt on 3¼mm (US3) needles.

BACK
Using 3mm (US2) needles and yarn A, cast on 157 sts. Work in twisted rib:
1st row (rs) K1 tbl, (P1, K1 tbl) to end.
2nd row P1, (K1 tbl, P1) to end.
Rep last 2 rows for 4cm (1½in), ending with a rs row. *Change to 3¼mm (US3) needles and cont in K2, P3 rib:
1st row (ws) P2, (K3, P2) to end.
2nd row K2, (P3, K2) to end.
Work 1 more row, inc 1 st at end of row. 158 sts. Commence colour patt, keep rib sections correct and use separate lengths of yarn for each colour, twisting yarns tog at colour joins to avoid holes.
1st row (rs) Rib 21A, K2B, (K2B, rib 24A, K2B) to last 23 sts, K2B, rib 21A.
2nd row Rib 19A, P4B, (P4B, rib 20A, P4B) to last 23 sts, P4B, rib 19A.
3rd row K1B, rib 16A, K6B, (K6B, rib 16A, K6B) to last 23 sts, K6B, rib 16A, K1B.
4th row P2B, rib 14A, P7B, (P7B, rib 14A, P7B) to last 23 sts, P7B, P14A, P2B.
5th row K3B, rib 12A, K6B, K2C, (K2C, K6B, rib 12A, K6B, K2C) to last 23 sts, K2C, K6B, rib 12A, K3B.
6th row P5B, rib 8A, P6B, P4C, (P4C, P6B, rib 8A, P6B, P4C) to last 23 sts, P4C, P6B, rib 8A, P5B.
7th row K1C, K6B, rib 4A, K6B, K6C, (K6C, K6B, rib 4A, K6B, K6C) to last 23 sts, K6C, K6B, rib 4A, K6B, K1C.

work in st st throughout

■ = A
⊠ = B
▣ = C
⊞ = D
◙ = E
◿ = F
◺ = G
⊓ = H
⊟ = J
◣ = L
▼ = M
◥ = N
◢ = Q
⊤ = R
⊐ = S
◪ = U
◹ = V

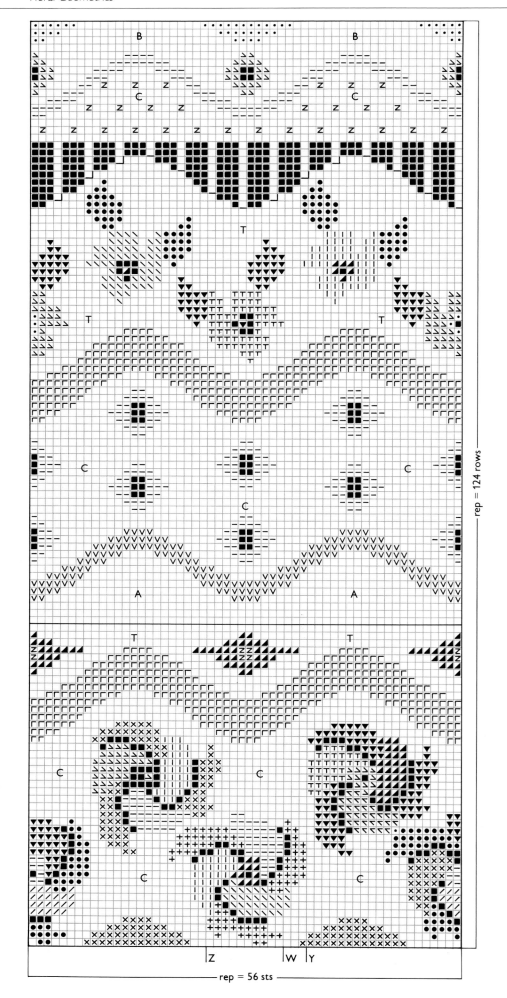

rep = 124 rows

rep = 56 sts

Now, beg with a P row, cont to work in st st and colour patt from chart.
1st row (ws) Beg at W, work 23 sts, rep 56 sts of 1st row to last 23 sts, then work to Z.
2nd row (rs) Beg at Z, work 23 sts, rep 56 sts of 2nd row to last 23 sts, then work to W.*
Cont in this way, keeping chart patt correct, dec 1 st at each end of 13th and every foll 15th row until 144 sts rem.
Now work straight until 153 rows have been worked from chart, ending with a P row.

Shape armholes
Cast off 7 sts at beg of next 2 rows. Dec 1 st at each end of next and every foll alt row until 126 sts rem.
Now cont straight until work measures 21cm (8¼in) from beg of armhole shaping, ending with a P row.

Shape shoulders
Cast off 13 sts at beg of next 2 rows and 15 sts at beg of foll 4 rows. Cast off rem 40 sts.

RIGHT FRONT
Using 3mm (US2) needles and yarn A, cast on 75 sts. Work 4cm (1½in) in twisted rib as given for back, ending with a rs row. Change to 3¼mm (US3) needles and cont in K2, P3 rib:
1st row (ws) (P2, K3) to end.
2nd row (P3, K2) to end.
These 2 rows form the rib. Work 1 more row, inc 1 st at beg of row. 76 sts.
Commence colour patt, keeping rib sections correct.
1st row (rs) (K2B, rib 24A, K2B) to last 20 sts, K2B, rib 18A.
2nd row Rib 16A, P4B, (P4B, rib 20A, P4B) to end.
3rd row (K6B, rib 16A, K6B) to last 20 sts, K6B, rib 14A.
4th row Rib 13A, P7B, (P7B, rib 14A, P7B) to end.
5th row (K2C, K6B, rib 12A, K6B, K2C) to last 20 sts, K2C, K6B, rib 12A.
6th row P2B, rib 8A, P6B, P4C, (P4C, P6B, rib 8A, P6B, P4C) to end.
7th row (K6C, K6B, rib 4A, K6B, K6C) to last 20 sts, K6C, K6B, rib 4A, K4B.
Now, beg with a P row, cont to work in st st and colour patt from chart.
1st row (ws) Beg at Y, work 20 sts, then work 56 sts of 1st row of chart.
2nd row Work 56 sts of 2nd row of chart, then work to Y.
Cont in this way, keeping chart correct, *at the same time* dec 1 st at side edge of 13th and every foll 15th row until 69 sts rem.
Now work straight until work matches back to armhole, ending at side edge.

Shape armhole and neck
Cast off 7 sts at beg of next row, then dec 1 st at armhole edge on 2 foll alt rows, *at the same time* dec 1 st at neck edge on next and every foll 4th row until 43 sts rem.
Cont straight until work matches back to shoulder shaping, ending at armhole edge.

Shape shoulder
Cast off 13 sts at beg of next row and 15 sts at beg of foll alt row. Work 1 row.
Cast off rem 15 sts.

LEFT FRONT
Work as given for right front, reversing all shapings.

SLEEVES
Using 3mm (US2) needles and yarn A, cast on 67 sts. Work 15cm (5¾in) in twisted rib as given for back, ending with a rs row.

Inc row (ws) Rib 7, (inc in each of next 2 sts, rib 1) 17 times, inc in next st, rib 8. 102 sts.
Work 3 rows in K2, P3 rib as given for back, ending with a rs row.
Now work as given for back from * to *.
Cont straight in this way until 121 rows have been worked from chart, ending with a P row.

Shape sleeve top
Cast off 7 sts at beg of next 2 rows and 2 sts at beg of next 6 rows. Dec 1 st at each end of next and every foll alt row until 70 sts rem, then at each end of every row until 58 sts rem.
Now dec 1 st at each end of every foll 3rd row until 32 sts rem, ending with a P row.
Cast off 8 sts at beg of next 2 rows. Cast off rem 16 sts.

FRONT BAND
Join shoulder seams.
Using 3mm (US2) needles and yarn A, cast on 11 sts. Work in twisted rib as given for back until band, when slightly stretched, fits up left front edge to neck shaping.
Pin band in position. Place 9 button markers on band, one 2cm (¾in) from cast-on edge and one at beg of neck shaping, with rem 7 spaced evenly between.
Now cont in rib until band is long enough to fit up left front neck, across back neck and down entire right front edge, making buttonholes to correspond with button markers as foll:
1st buttonhole row (rs) Rib 4, cast off 3 sts, rib to end.
2nd buttonhole row Rib to end, casting on 3 sts over those cast off in previous row.
Cast off in rib.

TO MAKE UP
Sew on front band.
Set in sleeves. Join side and sleeve seams, reversing cuff seam to fold back.
Sew on buttons.

The Wavy Fair Isle
pullover is worked in rich
winy colours – plum,
claret, port, burgundy. The
cardigan (far left) is a
heather blue version of
Oriental Poppies (page 12).

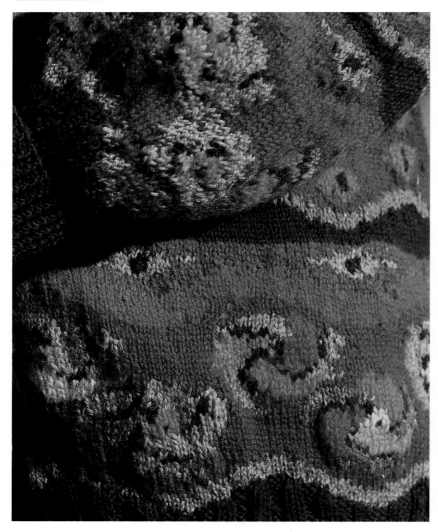

A detail of the Wavy Fair Isle sweater.

3rd row (K6B, rib 16A, K6B) to end.
4th row (P7B, rib 14A, P7B) to end.
5th row (K2C, K6B, rib 12A, K6B, K2C) to end.
6th row (P4C, P6B, rib 8A, K6B, P4C) to end.
7th row (K6C, K6B, rib 4A, K6B, K6C) to end.
Now, beg with a P row, cont to work in st st from chart on page 52 working 56 st rep across row.
*Work 109 rows, ending with a P row.
Shape armholes
Cast off 5 sts at beg of next 2 rows. Dec 1 st at each end of next and every foll alt row until 148 sts rem. **
Now work straight until work measures 24cm (9½in) from beg of armhole shaping, ending with a P row.
Shape shoulders
Cast off 14 sts at beg of next 4 rows and 13 sts at beg of foll 2 rows.
Cast off rem 66 sts.

FRONT
Work as given for back to **.
Now cont straight until work measures 12 rows fewer than back to shoulder shaping, ending with a P row.
Shape neck
Next row Patt 59 sts and turn leaving rem sts on a spare needle.
Next row Sl 1, P2 tog, psso, patt to end.
Next row Patt to last 3 sts, K3 tog.
Rep last 2 rows until 41 sts rem. Work 2 rows straight, ending with a P row.
Shape shoulder
Cast off 14 sts at beg of next and foll alt row.
Work 1 row. Cast off rem 13 sts.
With rs of work facing, return to sts on spare needle, rejoin yarn and cast off centre 30 sts, patt to end. 59 sts.
Next row Patt to last 3 sts, P3 tog tbl.
Next row Sl 1, K2 tog, psso, patt to end.
Rep last 2 rows until 41 sts rem. Work 3 rows straight, ending with a K row.
Shape shoulder
Work as given for first side.

SLEEVES
Using 3mm (US2) needles and yarn A, cast on 57 sts.
Work in K2, P3 rib as given for back for 13cm (5in), ending with a 2nd row, dec 1 st at end of last row. 56 sts.
Change to 3¼mm (US3) needles. Work as given for back from * to *. Inc and work into patt 1 st at each end of next and every foll alt row until there are 88 sts, then inc 1 st at each end of every foll 3rd row until there are 134 sts.
Cont straight until 109 rows have been worked from chart, ending with a P row.
Shape sleeve top
Cast off 5 sts at beg of next 2 rows. Dec 1 st at each end of next and every foll alt row until 114 sts rem, ending with a P row.
Cast off.

COLLAR
Using 3mm (US2) needles and yarn A, cast on 157 sts. Work in K2, P3 rib as given for back for 8cm (3in), ending with a 2nd row.
Cast off in rib.

TO MAKE UP
Join shoulder seams. Sew cast-on edge of collar around neck edge, beg and ending at centre front neck. Neatly join front edges for 4 rows.
Set in sleeves. Join side and sleeve seams.

SWEATER

SIZE
To fit one size only up to 107cm (42in) bust
Actual width measurement 120cm (47¼in)
Length to shoulder 67cm (26½in)
Sleeve seam 46cm (18in)

MATERIALS
200g (8oz) 4-ply in main colour (A)
100g (4oz) in 1 contrast colour (C)
50g (2oz) in each of 4 contrast colours (B, J, S, T)
25g (1oz) in each of 12 contrast colours
    (D, E, F, G, H, L, M, N, Q, R, U, V)
1 pair each 3mm (US2) and 3¼mm (US3) needles

TENSION
28 sts and 35 rows to 10cm (4in) over chart patt on 3¼mm (US3) needles.

BACK
Using 3mm (US2) needles and yarn A, cast on 167 sts.
Work in K2, P3 rib as foll:
1st row (rs) K2, (P3, K2) to end.
2nd row P2, (K3, P2) to end.
Rep last 2 rows for 10cm (4in), ending with a 2nd row, inc 1 st at end of last row. 168 sts.
Change to 3¼mm (US3) needles. *Commence colour patt; keep rib sections correct and use separate lengths of yarn for each colour area, twisting yarns tog at colour joins to avoid holes.
1st row (rs) (K2B, rib 24A, K2B) to end.
2nd row (P4B, rib 20A, P4B) to end.

Navajo

I wanted to get away from the usual fluid flower shapes, so I dropped this fairly stylized pelargonium into a patchwork of hard-edged geometrics taken from Navajo rugs.

CHART 1

rep = 105 rows

rep for sleeve = 36 sts

sleeve

rep for fronts = 75 sts

rep for back = 75 sts

back

SIZE
To fit one size only up to 91cm (36in) bust
Actual width measurement 97.5cm (38¼in)
Length to shoulder 55cm (21½in)
Sleeve seam 47cm (18½in)

MATERIALS
250g (10oz) 4-ply in main colour (A)
50g (2oz) in 1 contrast colour (F)
25g (1oz) in each of 19 contrast colours
   (B, C, D, E, G, H, J, L, M, N, Q, R, S, T, U, V,
   W, X, Y)
1 pair each 2¾mm (US2) and 3mm (US2) needles
2.50mm (USC) crochet hook
9 buttons

TENSION
32 sts and 42 rows to 10cm (4in) over chart patt
on 3mm (US2) needles.

BACK
Using 2¾mm (US2) needles and yarn A, cast on
156 sts. Work 5cm (2in) in K1, P1 rib.
Change to 3mm (US2) needles. Commence rib,
garter st and st st colour patt from chart 1; use
separate lengths of yarn for each colour area,
twisting yarns tog at colour joins to avoid holes.
Work 105 rows of chart, then work 1st-21st rows
again, *beg* and ending with a ws row.
Shape armholes
Keeping chart patt correct, dec 1 st at each end of
next 6 rows. 144 sts.
Now work straight until 210 rows have been
worked from chart, ending with a ws row.
Cast off.

LEFT FRONT
Using 2¾mm (US2) needles and yarn A, cast on 75
sts.
1st row (rs) K1, (P1, K1) to end.
2nd row P1, (K1, P1) to end.
Rep the last 2 rows until work measures 5cm (2in)
from cast-on edge, ending with a ws row.
Change to 3mm (US2) needles and commence rib,
garter st and st st colour patt from chart 1.
Work 105 rows of chart, then work 1st-21st rows
again, *beg* and ending with a ws row.
Shape armhole
Keeping chart correct, dec 1 st at armhole edge of
next 3 rows. 72 sts.
Now cont straight until 175 rows have been
worked from chart, ending with à rs row. **,
Shape neck
Cast off 36 sts at beg of next row, then cont
straight until 210 rows have been worked from
chart, ending with a ws row.
Cast off rem 36 sts.

RIGHT FRONT
Work as given for left front to **.
Work 1 row, then complete as given for left front.

SLEEVES
Using 2¾mm (US2) needles and yarn A, cast on 64
sts. Work 8cm (3in) in K1, P1 rib, end with a rs
row.
Inc row Rib1, *inc in next st, rib 5; rep from * to
last 3 sts, inc in next st, rib 2. 75 sts.
Change to 3mm (US2) needles and work in colour
patt from chart 1, *at the same time* inc and work
into K1, P1 rib and yarn A 1 st at each end of every
3rd row until there are 99 sts. Work 1 row
straight, ending with a rs row (37 rows have been
worked from chart).
Now cont in yarn A only and rib.

Next row (ws) (P1, K1, P1, K3) to last 3 sts, P1, K1,
P1.
Next row Inc in 1st st, P1, K1, (P3, K1, P1, K1) to last
6 sts, P3, K1, P1, inc in last st. 101 sts.
Cont in rib as set, inc 1 st at each end of every foll
3rd row until there are 141 sts.
Cont straight until work measures 44cm (17¼in)
from beg, ending with a ws row. Now work in K1,
P1 rib and st st from chart 2, work 10 rows. Work
2 rows st st in yarn A. Cast off.

*A detail of the metallic
grey cotton version of the
Navajo cardigan.*

work in st st throughout

⊡ = using A, K on ws rows
        P on ws rows
☐ = A unless otherwise
        indicated

■ = B	⊿ = M
⨆ = C	◤ = N
◢ = D	⩔ = Q
◣ = E	⊟ = S
⊞ = F	⊠ = U
⧄ = H	⊤ = V
⊡ = J	⊡ = X
⊞ = L	⊡ = Y

CHART 2

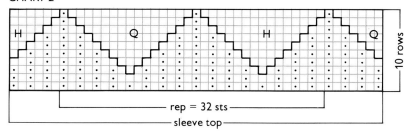

rep = 32 sts
sleeve top
10 rows

BUTTON BAND

Using 2¾mm (US2) needles and yarn A, cast on 11 sts. Cont in K1, P1 rib as given for left front until band, when slightly stretched, fits up right front to neck edge, ending with a ws row. Do not cut yarn. Leave sts on a holder.
Place 8 button markers on button band, the first 2cm (¾in) from cast-on, the last 2cm (¾in) below neck, with rem 6 evenly spaced between.

BUTTONHOLE BAND

Work as given for button band but cut yarn and leave sts on a holder and make buttonholes opposite markers as foll:
1st buttonhole row (rs) Rib 4, cast off 3, rib to end.
2nd buttonhole row Rib to end, casting on 3 sts over those cast off in previous row.

NECKBANDS

Join shoulder seams. Sew on front bands.
Right neck
With rs of work facing, using 2¾mm (US2) needles and yarn A, rib 11 sts from button band, K up 36 sts across front neck, 1 st from corner, K up 28 sts up right side of neck. 65 sts.
1st row (ws) (P1, K1) to 2 sts before corner st, P2 tog, P1, P2 tog tbl, (K1, P1) to end.
Cont in rib as set, work a further 14 rows dec 1 st at each side of corner st on every row.
Cast off in rib.
Left neck
With rs of work facing, using 2¾mm needles and yarn A, K up 28 sts from left side of neck, 1 st from corner, K up 36 sts across front neck then rib 11 sts from buttonhole band. 65 sts.
Work 9 rows as given for right neck.
1st buttonhole row Work to last 7 sts, cast off 3, rib to end.
2nd buttonhole row Work to end, casting on 3 sts over those cast off in previous row.
Work 4 rows as before. Cast off in rib.

NECK EDGING

Sew ends of neckbands to back neck. Using 2.50mm (USC) crochethook and yarn A, work crochet picot edging as foll:
1st row Work in double crochet around neck edge.
2nd row *1 double crochet into each of next 3 double crochet, 4 chain, slip st into last double crochet; rep from *

TO MAKE UP

Set in sleeves. Join side and sleeve seams. Sew on buttons.

The Navajo cardigan in its grey version (left) and in the oyster colourway (page 57) is worked in mercerized cotton, but would be equally nice in 4-ply wool.

Cables and Flowers

Climbing Roses

The twisted ogee cable echoes the rather formal pink roses in a design loosely based on an early Victorian wallpaper design. The main yarn used in the cream colourway is a mixture of wool and silk, which gives it a slight sheen.

SIZE
To fit one size only up to 81cm (32in) bust
Actual width measurement 88cm (34½in)
Length to shoulder 66cm (26in)
Sleeve seam 43cm (17in) with cuff folded back

MATERIALS
600g (24oz) four-ply yarn in main colour (A)
25g (1oz) in each of 11 contrast colours
    (B, C, D, E, F, G, H, J, L, M, N)
1 pair each 2¾mm (US2) and 3mm (US2) needles
Cable needle
2.50mm (USC) crochet hook

TENSION
40 sts and 40 rows to 10cm (4in) over chart patts
on 3mm (US2) needles.

SPECIAL ABBREVIATIONS
cross 4 left – sl 2 sts on to cable needle, hold at front, P2, K2 from cable needle
cross 4 right – sl 2 sts on to cable needle, hold at back, K2, P2 from cable needle
cross 3 left – sl 2 sts on to cable needle, hold at front, P1, K2 from cable needle
cross 3 right – sl 1 st on to cable needle, hold at back, K2, P1 from cable needle
cable 4 front – sl 2 sts on to cable needle, hold at front, K2, K2 from cable needle
cable 4 back – sl 2 sts on to cable needle, hold at back, K2, K2 from cable needle

BACK
Using 2¾mm (US2) needles and yarn A, cast on 177 sts.

Work in K1, P1 rib as foll:
1st row (rs) K1, (P1, K1) to end.
2nd row P1, (K1, P1) to end.
Rep the last 2 rows 3 times more, then 1st row again.
Change to 3mm (US2) needles and commence cable patt:
1st row (ws) *P1, K1, P1, reading from left to right work 1st row of chart 1; rep from * to last 3 sts, P1, K1, P1.
2nd row *K1, P1, K1, reading from right to left work 2nd row of chart 1; rep from * to last 3 sts, K1, P1, K1.
These 2 rows establish the patt. Cont as set until 64 rows have been worked from chart 1, ending with a rs row.
Now cont in flower and cable patt; use separate lengths of yarn for each colour area and twist yarns tog at colour joins to avoid holes. (Use diagram below to help with placing of chart patts.)
1st row (ws) Reading all charts from left to right, *PIA, KIA, PIA, work 1st row of chart 1, PIA, KIA, PIA, work 1st row of chart 2, PIA, KIA, PIA*, work 1st row of chart 1, PIA, KIA, PIA, work 1st row of chart 3, rep from * to * again.
2nd row (rs) Reading all charts from right to left, *KIA, PIA, KIA, work 2nd row of chart 2, KIA, PIA, KIA, work 2nd row of chart 1, KIA, PIA, KIA, work 2nd row of chart 3, KIA, PIA, KIA, work 2nd row of chart 1, then rep from * to * again.
3rd–32nd rows Cont as set until 32 rows have been worked from charts, ending with a rs row. **
33rd row Reading all charts from left to right, *PIA, KIA, PIA, work 1st row of chart 4, PIA,

Worked in a lovely soft silk-wool yarn, this cabled cream pullover is perfect for spring and early summer. One large deep pocket placed just off-centre is edged with a rolled ribbed top to echo the collar.

☐ = using A, K on rs rows, P on ws rows

⊡ = using A, P on rs rows, K on ws rows

⧅⧅ = cross 4 left

⧄⧄ = cable 4 front

⬒⬓ = cross 3 left

⧄⧄ = cross 4 right

⧅⧅ = cable 4 back

⧄⧄ = cross 3 right

CHART 1

1st row (ws)

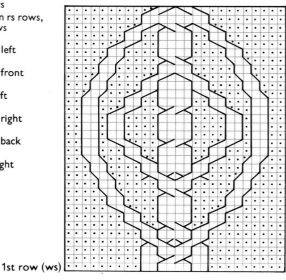

back

work in st st unless
otherwise indicated

☐ = using A, K on rs rows,
      P on ws rows
⊡ = using A, P on rs rows,
      K on ws rows
Ⓥ = B
⊠ = C
◉ = D
◩ = E
◨ = F
⊟ = G
⊞ = H
◪ = J
■ = L
Ⅱ = M
◺ = N

CHART 2

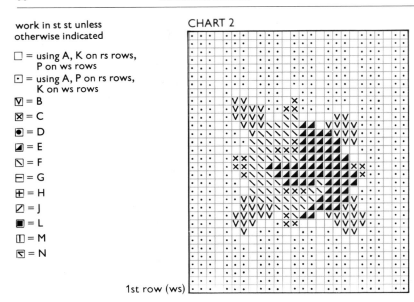

1st row (ws)

CHART 3

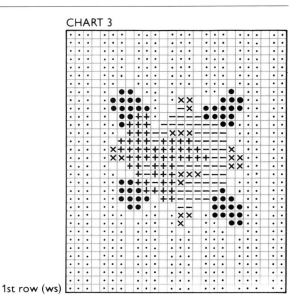

1st row (ws)

CHART 4

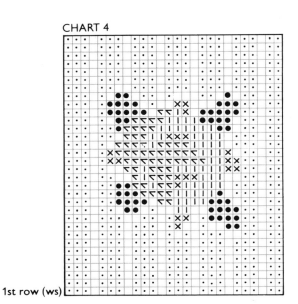

1st row (ws)

CHART 5

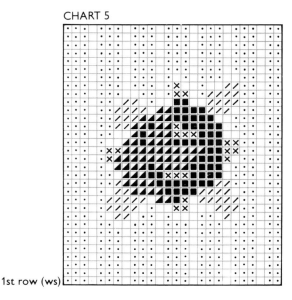

1st row (ws)

KIA, PIA, work 1st row of chart 1, PIA, KIA, PIA,
work 1st row of chart 5, PIA, KIA, PIA, work 1st
row of chart 1, rep from * to * again.
***34th row Reading all charts from right to left,
*KIA, PIA, KIA, work 2nd row of chart 1, KIA,
PIA, KIA, work 2nd row of chart 4, KIA, PIA,
KIA,*, work 2nd row of chart 1, KIA, PIA, KIA,
work 2nd row of chart 5, rep from * to * again.
35th-64th rows Cont as set until 32 rows have
been worked from charts.
These 64 rows form the flower and cable patt.
Shape armholes
Keeping patt correct, cast off 7 sts at beg of next 2
rows, then dec 1 st at beg of next 10 rows. 153 sts.
***
Cont without shaping until 192 rows of flower and
cable patt have been worked, ending with a rs row.
Cast off.

POCKET LINING
Using 3mm (US2) needles and yarn A, cast on 44
sts. Beg with a K row, work 70 rows st st.
Next row (K3, inc in next st) to last 4 sts, K4. 54
sts. Cut yarn and leave sts on a spare needle.

FRONT
Work as given for back to **.
Place pocket
Cont working in patt as given for back:
Next row (33rd patt row) (ws) Patt 89, sl next 54
sts on to a holder, patt across sts of pocket lining,
patt to end. 177 sts.
Now work as given for back from *** to ***.
Cont without shaping until 176 rows of flower and
cable patt have been worked, ending with a rs row.
Shape neck
Next row (ws) Patt 60 sts and leave on a spare
needle, cast off 33 sts, patt to end.
Cont on these 60 sts for left side of neck.
Dec 1 st at neck edge on every row until 46 sts
rem. Work 1 row, ending with same patt row as
back. Cast off.
With rs facing, return to sts on spare needle, rejoin
yarn at neck edge and work to match first side of
neck.

SLEEVES
Worked from top to cuff.
Using 3mm (US2) needles and yarn A, cast on 175
sts. Cont in cable and rib patt, using diagram above

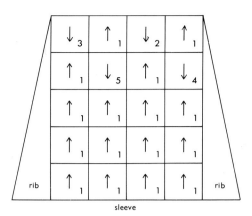

sleeve

to help place charts:
1st row (ws) (P1, K3) 7 times, (P1, K1, P1, reading from left to right, work 1st row of chart 1) 4 times, P1, K1, P1, (K3, P1) 7 times.
2nd row (rs) (K1, P3) 7 times, (K1, P1, K1, reading from right to left, work 2nd row of chart 1) 4 times, K1, P1, K1, (P3, K1) 7 times.
These 2 rows establish the cable and rib patt. Cont until 32 rows have been worked from chart, ending with a rs row.
Cont in patt as set, dec 1 st at each end of next and every foll 4th row until 143 sts rem.
Work 3 rows straight (96 rows have been worked in cable and rib patt).
Next row (ws) K2A tog, K2A, (P1A, K3A) twice, *P1A, K1A, P1A, reading from left to right work 1st row of chart 1, P1A, K1A, P1A*, turn chart 5 upside down, reading from left to right work 32nd row, rep from * to * again, turn chart 4 upside down, reading from left to right work 32nd row, P1A, K1A, P1A, (K3A, P1A) twice, K2A, K2A tog.
This row sets position of charts and direction of working, cont as set until 32 chart rows have been worked, *at the same time* dec 1 st at each end of every foll 4th row. 127 sts.
Next row (ws) K2A tog, K2A, P1A, K1A, P1A, turn chart 3 upside down, reading from left to right work 32nd row, *P1A, K1A, P1A, reading from left to right work 1st row of chart 1, P1A, K1A, P1A*, turn chart 2 upside down, reading from left to right work 32nd row, rep from * to * again, K2A, K2A tog.
This row sets position of charts and direction of working, cont as set, *at the same time* dec 1 st at each end of every foll 4th row until 117 sts rem.
Cont without shaping until 32 chart rows have been worked, ending with a rs row. Cont in yarn A only.
Next row P1, (P2 tog) to end. 59 sts.
Change to 2¾mm needles and, beg with a 2nd

row, work 10cm (4 in) K1, P1 rib as given for back. Cast off in rib.

POCKET TOP
With rs facing, using 2¾mm needles and yarn A, return to 54 sts on holder.
1st row K1, P2, (K3, P2) to last st, K1.
2nd row P1, K2, (P3, K2) to last st, P1.
Rep last 2 rows 6 times more, then 1st row again.
Cast off 6 sts at beg of next and 7 foll alt rows.
Work 1 row.
Cast off rem 6 sts.

COLLAR
Using 2¾mm needles and yarn A, cast on 155 sts.
1st row (rs) K1, (P3, K2) to last 4 sts, P3, K1.
2nd row P1, (K3, P2) to last 4 sts, K3, P1.
Rep the last 2 rows until collar measures 7cm (2¾in) from cast-on edge, ending with a ws row.
Cast off.

TO MAKE UP
Join shoulder seams.
Set in sleeves, easing to fit, joining cast-off sts at underarm to final rows of sleeve top, and reversing cuff seam to fold back. Join side and sleeve seams.
Fold pocket top over on to rs and sew down edges. Catch down pocket lining on ws.
Sew on collar, starting and ending at centre front neck.
Collar edging
Using 2.50mm (USC) crochet hook and yarn A, work crochet picot edging as foll:
1st row Work in double crochet around collar edge.
2nd row *1 double crochet into each of next 3 double crochet, 4 chain, slip st into last double crochet; rep from *.

(Overleaf) In the soft mole grey version of Climbing Roses I have used contrasting colours behind each flower.

Orange Blossom

The first version of this design was the brick pink colourway on page 74, which closely reflected the actual flowers I'd drawn it from, but then I experimented with more vibrant tones and a longer looser shape which produced the cardigan shown here.

SIZE
To fit one size only up to 107cm (42in) bust
Actual width measurement 121cm (47½in)
Length to shoulder 70cm (27½in)
Sleeve seam 48cm (18¾in)

MATERIALS
450g (18oz) 4-ply in main colour (A)
50g (2oz) in each of 2 contrast colours (C, G)
25g (1oz) in each of 7 contrast colours
   (B, D, E, F, H, J, L)
1 pair each 3mm (US2) and 3¼mm (US3) needles
3mm (US2) circular needle
Cable needle
9 buttons

SPECIAL ABBREVIATION
C4F – sl next 2 sts on to cable needle and hold at front, K2, then K2 from cable needle

TENSION
26 sts and 34 rows to 10cm (4in) over chart patt on 3¼mm (US3) needles.

CABLE PANEL
Worked in yarn A over 8 sts.
1st row (rs) P2, K4, P2.
2nd row K2, P4, K2.
3rd-8th rows Rep 1st-2nd rows 3 times more.
9th row P2, C4F, P2.
10th row As 2nd row.
These 10 rows form cable panel.

BACK
Using 3mm (US2) needles and yarn A, cast on 182 sts.
Work 10 rows in K1, P1 rib.
Change to 3¼mm (US3) needles and commence cable and colour patt; use separate lengths of yarn for each colour area, twisting yarns tog at colour joins to avoid holes.
1st row (rs) K8A, (work 1st row cable panel) 3 times, K12A, work 1st row of cable panel, K2A, (work 1st row of chart) twice, K2A, work 1st row cable panel, K12A, (work 1st row cable panel) 3 times, K8A.
2nd row P8A, (work 2nd row cable panel) 3 times, P12A, work 2nd row cable panel, P2A, (work 2nd row of chart) twice, P2A, work 2nd row cable panel, P12A, (work 2nd row cable panel) 3 times, P8A.
These 2 rows set the cable and colour patt with st st edge sts.
Keeping patt correct, work a further 144 rows, ending with a ws row.
Shape armholes
Cast off 14 sts at beg of next 2 rows. 154 sts.
Now work 68 rows straight ending with a ws row.
Cont in yarn A only, keeping cable and st st patt correct but working P5, K1 rib as set over 37 chart sts.
Work 12 rows, ending with a ws row.
Cast off.

LEFT FRONT
Using 3mm (US2) needles and yarn A, cast on 82 sts.
Work 10 rows in K1, P1 rib, inc 1 st at side edge of last row. 83 sts.
Change to 3¼mm (US3) needles and commence patt. ******
1st row (rs) K8A, (work 1st row of cable panel) 3 times, K2A, work 1st row of chart, K2A, work 1st row of cable panel, K2A.
2nd row P2A, work 2nd row of cable panel, P2A, work 2nd row of chart, P2A, (work 2nd row of cable panel) 3 times, P8A.
These 2 rows set the cable and colour patt with st st edge sts.
Keeping patt correct, work a further 144 rows, ending with a ws row.
Shape armhole
Cast off 14 sts at beg of next row. 69 sts.
Now work 11 rows straight.

☐ = using A, K on rs rows, P on ws rows
⊡ = using A, P on rs rows, K on ws rows
☒ = B
◩ = C
⊞ = D
◺ = E
⊙ = F
⊡ = G
■ = H
◣ = J
◿ = L

Shape neck
Dec 1 st at neck edge on next and every foll 3rd row until 45 sts rem, ending with a ws row.
Cast off.

RIGHT FRONT
Work right front exactly as given for left front to **
1st row (rs) K2A, work 1st row of cable panel, K2A, work 1st row of chart, K2A, (work 1st row of cable panel) 3 times, K8A.
2nd row P8A, (work 2nd row of cable panel) 3 times, P2A, work 2nd row of chart, P2A, work 2nd row of cable panel, P2A.
These 2 rows set the cable and colour patt with st st edge sts.
Keeping patt correct, work a further 145 rows, ending with a rs row.

Shape armhole
Complete as given for left front working 1 row less before neck shaping.

SLEEVES
Using 3mm (US2) needles and yarn A, cast on 51 sts.
1st row (rs) K1, (P1, K1) to end.
2nd row P1, (K1, P1) to end.
Rep last 2 rows for 10cm (4in), ending with a ws row.
Inc row Rib 5, (inc in next st, rib 3) 10 times, inc in next st, rib 5. 62 sts.
Inc row Rib 2, (inc in next st, rib 2) 19 times, inc in next st, rib 2. 82 sts.
Change to 3¼mm (US3) needles and commence patt:
Next row P4A, (work 1st row of chart) twice, P4A.
Next row K4A, (work 2nd row of chart) twice, K4A.
These 2 rows establish the patt.
Cont as set, inc and work into P5, K1 rib and yarn A, 1 st at each end of next and every foll 5th row until there are 134 sts. Cont straight until 144 rows have been worked from chart, ending with a ws row.
Cast off.

BUTTON BAND AND HALF COLLAR
Join shoulder seams.
Using 3mm (US2) needles and yarn A, cast on 11 sts.
1st row (rs) K1 tbl, (P1, K1 tbl) to end.
2nd row P1, (K1 tbl, P1) to end.
Rep last 2 rows until left front band, when slightly stretched, fits up to beg of front neck shaping, ending at inner front edge. Inc and work into rib 1 st at outer edge of every foll row until there are 28 sts.
Cont straight until collar fits to centre back neck.
Cast off.
Place 9 button markers on button band, the first 7 rows from cast-on edge, the last 12 rows below beg of collar shaping, with rem 7 evenly spaced between.

BUTTONHOLE BAND AND HALF COLLAR
Work as given for button band, reversing shaping and making buttonholes opposite markers as foll:
1st buttonhole row (rs) Rib 4, cast off 3, rib to end of row.
2nd buttonhole row Rib to end, casting on 3 sts over those cast off in previous row.

TO MAKE UP
Sew on front bands and collar sections, neatly join centre back seam.
Collar edging
Using 3mm (US2) circular needle and yarn A, with rs of work facing, K up 190 sts evenly around straight edge of collar.
Work in rows.
Beg with a 2nd row, work 4 rows K1 tbl, P1 rib as given for button band, dec 1 st at each end of every row.
Cast off in rib.
Set in sleeves, sewing final rows to cast-off sts at underarms.
Join side and sleeve seams.
Sew on buttons.

work in st st unless otherwise indicated

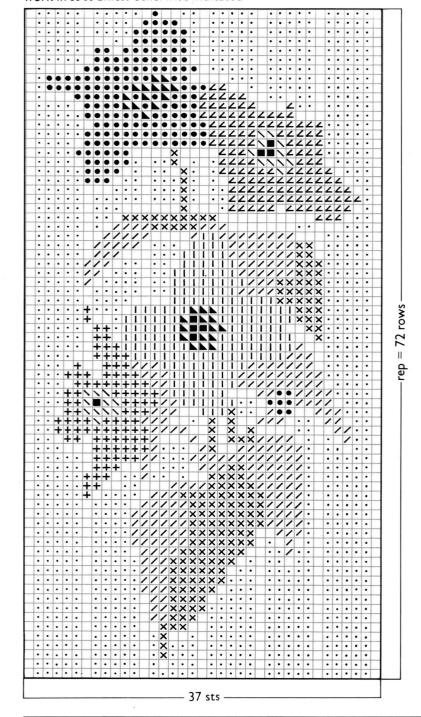

— 37 sts —

rep = 72 rows

Front detail of the Orange Blossom Cardigan.

The brick-red version of the Orange Blossom design.

Brocade

I called this design brocade because its alternating cable and richly coloured floral panels reminded me of those wonderful embossed Regency wallcoverings. The same design has been used for a pair of chunky socks (page 81).

CARDIGAN

SIZE
To fit one size only up to 96cm (38in) bust
Actual width measurement 106cm (41¾in)
Length to shoulder 65cm (25½in)
Sleeve seam 47.5cm (18¾in)

MATERIALS
500g (20oz) four-ply yarn in main colour (A)
50g (2oz) in 1 contrast colour (B)
25g (1oz) in each of 11 contrast colours
 (C, D, E, F, G, H, J, L, M, N, Q)
1 pair each 3mm (US2) and 3¼mm (US3) needles
Cable needle
9 buttons

TENSION
36 sts and 40 rows to 10cm (4in) over chart patt on 3¼mm (US3) needles

CABLE PANELS
Cable 1
Worked over 18 sts in yarn A.
1st row (rs) P1, K1, (P2, K2) 3 times, P2, K1, P1.
2nd and every alt row K1, P1, K2, (P2, K2) 3 times, P1, K1.
3rd and 5th rows As 1st row.
7th row P1, K1, P2, K2, P2, sl next 4 sts on to cable needle and hold at back, K2, then sl 2 P sts from cable needle back on to left-hand needle and P them, then K2 from cable needle, P2, K1, left-hand needle and P them, then K2 from cable needle, P2, K1, P1.

work in st st unless otherwise indicated

☐ = using A, K on rs rows, P on ws rows
⊡ = using A, P on rs rows, K on ws rows
◣ = B
⊟ = C
▼ = D
◫ = E
◢ = F
◉ = G
■ = H
☒ = J
◿ = L
⊤ = M
◪ = N
◺ = Q
⊞ = F on back and fronts, G on sleeve

CHART 1   **CHART 2**

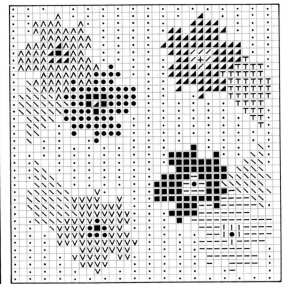

9th and 11th rows As 1st row.
13th row P1, K1, P2, sl next 4 sts on to cable
needle and hold at front, K2, then sl 2 P sts from
cable needle back on to left-hand needle and P.
them, then K2 from cable needle, P2, K2, P2, K1,
P1. The 2nd-13th rows form the patt rep.
Cable 2
Worked over 12 sts in yarn A.
1st row (rs) P3, K6, P3.
2nd and every alt row K3, P6, K3.
3rd row As 1st row.
5th row P3, sl next 3 sts on to cable needle and
hold at back, K3, then K3 from cable needle, P3.
6th row As 2nd row.
The 1st-6th rows form the patt rep.

BACK
Using 3mm (US2) needles and yarn A, cast on 202
sts. Work in K2, P2 rib as foll:
1st row (rs) K2, (P2, K2) to end.
2nd row P2, (K2, P2) to end.
Rep last 2 rows until work measures 5cm (2in)
ending with a ws row, inc 1 st at each end of last
row. 204 sts.
Change to 3¼mm (US3) needles and work in cable
and colour patt, using separate lengths of yarn for
each colour area, twisting yarns tog at colour joins
to avoid holes as foll:
1st row (rs) (Patt 1st row of chart 1, 1st row of
cable 1, 1st row of chart 2, 1st row of cable 2)
twice, 1st row of chart 1, 1st row of cable 1.
2nd row (Patt 2nd row of cable 1, 2nd row of
chart 1, 2nd row of cable 2, 2nd row of chart 2)
twice, 2nd row of cable 1, 2nd row of chart 1.
These 2 rows set the position of cable and colour
patt.
Cont as set until back measures 43cm (17in) from
cast-on edge, ending with a ws row.
Shape armholes
Cast off 5 sts at beg of next 2 rows, 3 sts at beg of
next 4 rows and 4 sts at beg of foll 4 rows. 166 sts.
Now work straight until back measures 22cm
(8½in) from beg of armhole shaping, ending with a
ws row. Cast off.

LEFT FRONT
Using 3mm (US2) needles and yarn A, cast on 102
sts.
Cont in K2, P2 rib as given for back until work
measures 5cm (2in), ending with a ws row. **
Change to 3¼mm (US3) needles and cable and
colour patt as foll:
1st row (rs) Patt 1st row of chart 1, 1st row of
cable 1, 1st row of chart 2, 1st row of cable 2, 1st
row of chart 1.
2nd row Patt 2nd row of chart 1, 2nd row of cable
2, 2nd row of chart 2, 2nd row of cable 1, 2nd row
of chart 1.
These 2 rows set the position of cable and colour
patt.
*** Cont as set until front measures 43cm (17in)
from cast-on edge, ending with a ws row.
Shape armhole
Cast off 5 sts at beg of next row, 3 sts at beg of
next 2 alt rows and 4 sts at beg of foll 2 alt rows.
83 sts. Now work straight until front measures
17cm (6¾in) from beg of armhole shaping, ending
with a rs row.
Shape neck
Cast off 17 sts at beg of next row, then dec 1 st at
neck edge on every row until 54 sts rem.
Work straight until front matches back to cast-off
edge. Cast off.

*The Brocade cardigan (right) with the black version of
the Auriculas cardigan (left, page 84).*

CHART 3

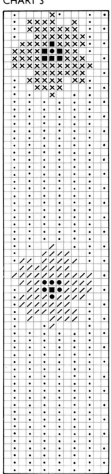

☐ = using A, K on rs rows,
     P on ws rows
⊡ = using A, P on rs rows,
     K on ws rows

◉ = G
◼ = H
☒ = J
▧ = L

RIGHT FRONT
Work as given for left front to **.
Change to 3¼mm (US3) needles and cable and colour patt as foll:
1st row (rs) Patt 1st row cable 1, 1st row of chart 2, 1st row of cable 2, 1st row of chart 1, 1st row of cable 1.
2nd row Patt 2nd row of cable 1, 2nd row of chart 1, 2nd row of cable 2, 2nd row of chart 2, 2nd row of cable 1.
These 2 rows set the position of cable and colour patt.
Complete as given for left front from ***, reversing shaping.

SLEEVES
(Worked from sleeve top to cuff.)
Using 3¼mm (US3) needles and yarn A, cast on 124 sts.
Work in cable and rib patt as foll:
1st row (rs) Beg at 5th st, patt 1st row of chart 2, 1st row of cable 2, 1st row of chart 1, 1st row of cable 1, 1st row of chart 2, then work 1st row of cable 2 to end.
This row sets position of cable and colour patts.
Shape top
Cast on 6 sts at beg of next 2 rows then cast on 4 sts at beg of every foll row until there are 168 sts, working extra sts at one side into rem sts of chart 2 then cable 1, and on the other side into rem sts of cable 2 then chart 1.
Cont as set, *at the same time* dec 1 st at each end of every foll 5th row until 110 sts rem.
Now work straight until sleeve measures 40cm (15¾in) from cast-on edge, ending with a ws row.
Change to 3mm (US2) needles and yarn A.
Next row (K2 tog) to last 2 sts, K2. 56 sts.
Work 10cm (4in) in K2, P2 rib.
Cast off in rib.

BUTTON BAND
Using 3mm (US2) needles and yarn A, cast on 14 sts.
Cont in rib as foll:
1st row (rs) (K1, P1) to last 2 sts, K2.
2nd row (K1, P1) to end.
Rep these 2 rows until band is long enough, when slightly stretched, to fit up left front to neck shaping, ending with a ws row.
Cast off in rib.
Place 9 button markers on button band, the first 5 rows from cast-on edge, the last 4 rows from cast-off edge, with rem 7 evenly spaced between.

BUTTONHOLE BAND
Using 3mm (US2) needles and yarn A, cast on 14 sts. Cont in rib as foll:
1st row (rs) K2, (P1, K1) to end.
2nd row (P1, K1) to end.
Rep last 2 rows once more.
1st buttonhole row Rib 6, cast off 2, rib to end.
2nd buttonhole row Rib to end, casting on 2 sts over those cast off in previous row.
Cont in rib as set, making 2nd buttonhole opposite marker.
Now cont to work from chart 3, rep 1st–64th rows *at the same time* making buttonholes opposite markers. When 9th buttonhole has been completed, work 4 rows rib and cast off in rib.

TO MAKE UP
Join shoulder seams.
Sew on buttonhole and button bands.
Neckband
Using 3mm (US2) needles and yarn A, with rs facing, K up 44 sts, across top of buttonhole band and up right side of neck, 43 sts across back neck and 44 sts down left side of neck and across button band. 131 sts.
1st row P2 tog, (P1, K1) to last 3 sts, P1, P2 tog.
2nd row K2 tog, (P1, K1) to last 3 sts, P1, K2 tog.
Cont in rib as set, work 3 more rows, dec 1 st at each end of every row.
Cast off in rib.
Set in sleeves, easing to fit. Join side and sleeve seams. Sew on buttons.

SOCKS

SIZE
Length from toe to heel 24.5cm (9½in)

MATERIALS
125g (5oz) 4-ply in main colour (A)
Oddments in each of 16 contrast colours (B,C,D,E,F,G,H,J,L,M,N,Q,R,S,T,U)
1 pair 2¾mm (US2) and 3mm (US2) needles
Cable needle

TENSION
32 sts and 40 rows to 10cm (4in) over chart patt on 3mm (US2) needles

CABLE PANEL
Worked throughout in yarn A over 19 sts.
1st row (rs) P2, K6, P3, K6, P2.
2nd row K2, P6, K3, P6, K2.
3rd–4th rows Rep 1st and 2nd rows again.
5th row P2, sl next 3 sts on to cable needle and hold at back, K3, then K3 from cable needle, P3, sl next 3 sts on to cable needle and hold at front, K3, then K3 from cable needle, P2.
6th row As 2nd row.
These 6 rows form the cable panel.

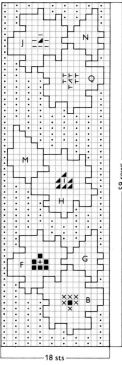

CHART 1

59 rows

18 sts

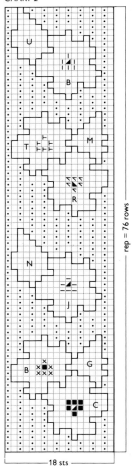

CHART 2

rep = 76 rows

18 sts

TO MAKE

Using 2¾mm (US2) needles and yarn A, cast on 75 sts. Cont in K2, P2 rib:

1st row (rs) K2, (P2, K2) to end.
2nd row P2, (K2, P2) to end.

Rep these 2 rows for 9cm (3½in) ending with a ws row.

Change to 3mm (US2) needles.

Commence cable panels and rib and colour patt from charts; use small separate lengths of yarn for each colour area, twisting yarns tog at colour joins to avoid holes.

1st row (rs) Work 1st row of chart 1, work 1st row of cable panel, work 1st row of chart 2, work 1st row of cable panel.

2nd row Work 2nd row of cable panel, work 2nd row of chart 2, work 2nd row of cable panel, work 2nd row of chart 1.

Cont in this way, keeping charts and cable panels correct.

Work a further 56 rows.

Divide for heel and instep

Next row Patt 55 sts and turn, leaving 19 sts on a holder.

Next row Patt 36 sts and turn, leaving 19 sts on a holder.

Cont on these 36 sts, keeping chart 2 and rem 18 sts of cable panel correct, work a further 74 rows, ending with a ws row.

Leave sts on a spare needle.

Now with rs of work facing, sl sts from both holders on to one needle, with back of leg seam at centre. 38 sts.

Cont in heel rib and yarn A only.

1st row (rs) (Sl 1, K1) to end.
2nd row K1, P to last st, K1.

These 2 rows form heel rib.

Rep them 19 times more.

Turn heel

1st row K28, sl 1, K1, psso, turn.
2nd row P19, P2 tog, turn.

3rd row K19, sl 1, K1, psso, turn.
4th row As 2nd row.

Rep last 2 rows until 20 sts rem, ending with a P row, then on to same needle, P up 16 sts along side of heel flap. 36 sts.

Next row K to end, then K up 16 sts along side of heel flap. 52 sts.

Next row P.

Now cont in heel rib and shape instep as foll:

1st row (rs) K1, sl 1, K1, psso, work in heel rib to last 3 sts, K2 tog, K1.

2nd row K1, P to last st, K1.

Rep last 2 rows until 40 sts rem, then cont in heel rib until foot section measures same as top section, ending with a ws row.

Next row Work to end, then work in heel rib across 36 sts on spare needle. 76 sts.

Next row K1, P to last st, K1.

Shape toe

1st row (rs) (K1, K2 tog, rib 32, K2 tog, K1) twice.
2nd and every alt row K1, P to last st, K1.
3rd row (K1, K2 tog, rib 30, K2 tog, K1) twice.
5th row (K1, K2 tog, rib 28, K2 tog, K1) twice.

Cont to dec in this way on alt rows until 32 sts rem, ending with a ws row.

Now sl first 16 sts on to a spare needle, fold work in half with rs facing and cast off both sets of sts tog or graft sts.

Work second sock in the same way.

TO MAKE UP

Join foot and tops sections.

Join back seam.

work in st st throughout unless otherwise indicated	⊞ = B	⊟ = H
	⊠ = C	⊟ = L
☐ = A, K on rs rows, P on ws rows	■ = D	◣ = R
⊡ = A, P on rs rows, K on ws rows	◢ = E	◁ = S
	⊡ = F	

Millefiori

Auriculas

Auriculas are fascinating plants – that mixture of soft mossy flowerheads and sage-coloured leaves was a great springboard for this design, which I've used here on a sweater and a cardigan. The sweater is worked in wool, and the bright colours on a black background and the side-buttoning neck detail give it an Oriental feel. The fine-ribbed sleeves of the short cotton cardigan have an undulating stripe background to the flower motif.

CARDIGAN

SIZE
To fit one size only up to 102cm (40in) bust
Actual width measurement 111.5cm (43¾in)
Length to shoulder 48.5cm (19in)
Sleeve seam 46cm (18in)

MATERIALS
300g (12oz) 4-ply in main colour (A)
100g (4oz) in 1 contrast colour (B)
50g (2oz) in 1 contrast colour (N)
25g (1oz) in each of 14 contrast colours
   (C, D, E, F, G, H, J, L, M, Q, R, S, T, U)
1 pair each 2¾mm (US2) and 3mm (US2) needles
2¾mm (US2) circular needle
6 buttons

TENSION
32 sts and 42 rows to 10cm (4in) over chart 2
colour patt on 3mm (US2) needles.

BACK
Using 2¾mm (US2) needles and yarn A, cast on
176 sts. Work 16 rows in K1, P1 rib.
Change to 3mm (US2) needles and commence
colour patt from chart 1 on page 86; use separate
lengths of yarn for each colour area and twist yarns
tog at colour joins to avoid holes. Work 22 rows
only, noting background must be worked entirely
in yarn A.
Now work in st st from chart 2 on page 86, with
edge sts in rib as foll:
Next row (rs) (K1A, P4A) 4 times, (work 1st row
of chart 2) twice, (P4A, K1A) 4 times.
Next row (ws) (P1A, K4A) 4 times, (work 2nd row
of chart 2) twice, (K4A, P1A) 4 times.
These 2 rows establish the position of chart 2 with
edge sts in rib.
Keeping chart correct, cont until 80 rows have
been worked from chart 2.
Shape armholes
Cont working as set, cast off 7 sts at beg of next 4
rows. Dec 1 st at each end of next and every foll
alt row until 136 sts rem.
Cont without further shaping until work measures
20.5cm (8in) from beg of armhole shaping, ending
with a ws row.

(Opposite) The creamy colourway of the Auriculas cotton cardigan.

SWEATER CHART 2

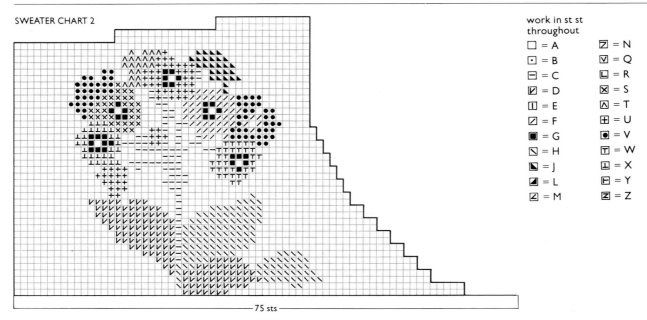

———— 75 sts ————

work in st st
throughout

□ = A	☑ = N	
⊡ = B	☑ = Q	
⊟ = C	▣ = R	
◩ = D	☒ = S	
◫ = E	◸ = T	
◪ = F	⊞ = U	
◼ = G	◉ = V	
◺ = H	◲ = W	
◣ = J	◳ = X	
◪ = L	⊟ = Y	
◪ = M	◪ = Z	

SWEATER CHART 3

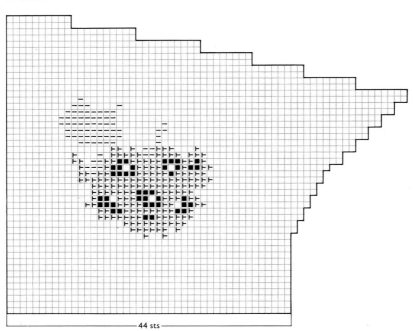

———— 44 sts ————

Now commence working from chart 2, cast off 8 sts at beg of next row then 5 sts at beg of foll alt row.
Cast off 2 sts at beg of 6 foll alt rows then dec 1 st at neck edge on every foll alt row until 44 sts rem.
Cont without shaping, work 11 rows.
Cont in yarn A only, work 1 row, ending at armhole edge.
Shape shoulder
Cast off 15 sts at beg of next and foll alt row.
Work 1 row.
Cast off rem 14 sts.

LEFT SHOULDER INSERT
Using 3¼mm (US3) needles and yarn A, cast on 14 sts.
Next row K.
Next row Cast on 15 sts, P to end.
Rep last 2 rows once more. 44 sts.
Now commence working from chart 3. Work 13 rows, then shape neck inc 1 st at end of next and 5 foll alt rows. Cast on 2 sts at beg of next and 5 foll alt rows. 62 sts. Work 1 row.
Now shape lower edge, cast off 8 sts at beg of

next and 3 foll alt rows.
Cast off 10 sts at beg of foll 2 alt rows. Work 1 row. Cast off rem 10 sts.

BUTTON BAND
With rs of work facing, using 2¾mm (US2) needles and yarn A, K up 62 sts evenly along lower edge of left shoulder insert.
Work 6 rows K1, P1 rib.
Cast off in rib.

SLEEVES
Using 2¾mm (US2) needles and yarn A, cast on 60 sts and work 11cm (4¼in) in K1, P1 rib.
Inc row (Rib twice into next st) to end. 120 sts.
Change to 3¼mm (US3) needles. Cont working in colour patt from from chart 4, *at the same time* inc and work into st st and yarn A 1 st at each end of every foll 10th row until there are 138 sts.
Now cont without further shaping until 132 rows have been worked from chart.
Cont in yarn A only, work 8 rows st st, ending with a ws row.
Cast off.

FRONT NECK EDGING

Join shoulder seams.

With rs of work facing, using 2¾mm (US2) circular needle and yarn X, K up 116 sts evenly along front neck edge, 43 sts across back neck and 40 sts down left front neck. 199 sts. Work in rows.

Change to 3¼mm (US3) circular needle.

Base row P to end.

Change to 2¾mm (US2) circular needle and work 5 rows st st beg with a K row.

Hem row (ws) Sl I, (P tog next st and loop of corresponding st in base row) to end.

Change to yarn A. K I row.

Cont in KI, PI rib, work 2 rows.

1st buttonhole row (ws) Rib 128, (cast off 3 sts, rib II including st used to cast off) 5 times, rib to end.

2nd buttonhole row Rib to end, casting on 3 sts over those cast off.

Rib 2 rows. Cast off in rib.

TO MAKE UP

Overlap front main piece over left shoulder insert and catch together ends of button bands.

Set in sleeves, joining cast-off sts at underarm to final rows of sleeve. Join side and sleeve seams. Sew on buttons.

SWEATER CHART 4

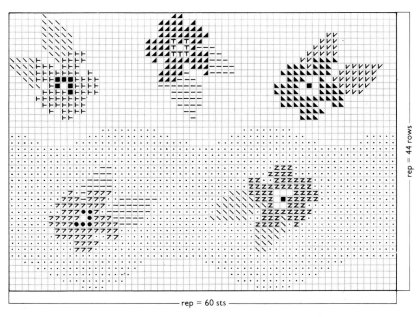

rep = 44 rows

rep = 60 sts

Chevron Floral

This long loose tunic is basically a single large chevron pattern, striped in bands of flowers in chalky pastels. It is worked from the neck down, and the ribbed yoke is knitted on afterwards.

SIZE
To fit one size only up to 102cm (40in) bust
Actual width measurement 120cm (47in)
Length to shoulder 67cm (26½in)
Sleeve seam 45.5cm (18in)

MATERIALS
200g (8oz) 4-ply in main colour (A)
75g (3oz) in 1 contrast colour (J)
50g (2oz) in each of 3 contrast colours (E, U, e)
25g (1oz) in each of 23 contrast colours
    (B, C, D, F, G, H, L, M, N, Q, R, S, T, U, V,
    W, X, Y, Z, a, b, d, f)
1 pair each 3mm (US2) and 3¼mm (US3)
    needles
3¼mm (US3) circular needle
2.50mm (USC) crochet hook

TENSION
28 sts and 36 rows to 10cm (4in) over colour patt on 3¼mm (US3) needles.

SPECIAL ABBREVIATION
M1 – with the right-hand needle pick up the bar between the last st and the next st and K it to make a st.

BACK
Beg at neck edge, using 3¼mm (US3) needles and yarn A, cast on 5 sts. Shape point in K1, P1 rib as foll:
Next row (ws) P1, (K1, P1) twice.
Next row Inc in first st, P1, M1, K1 (centre st), M1, P1, inc in last st. 9 sts.
Next row Inc in first st, rib 3, P1 (centre st), rib 3, inc in last st. 11 sts.
Next row Inc in first st, rib 4, M1, K1, M1, rib 4, inc in last st. 15 sts.

Next row Inc in first st, rib 6, P1, rib 6, inc in last st. 17 sts.
Cont to inc in this way until there are 33 sts, ending with a rs row.
Next row P twice into first st, P15, P centre st, P15, P twice into last st. 35 sts.
Now commence st st colour patt working sts either side of centre st from chart 1, shaping as shown; use separate lengths of yarn for each colour area and twist yarns tog at colour joins to avoid holes.
Read K and P rows from chart in the same way: work every chart row firstly from right to left, K or P the centre st in background colour (note, this st is not shown on chart), then work same row again from left to right.
1st row (rs) Using yarn B, inc in first st, K2C, K14B, M1 in yarn B, K1B (centre st), M1 in yarn B, K14B, K2C, using yarn B, inc in last st. 39 sts.
2nd row Using yarn B, inc in first st, P5C, P13B, P1B (centre st), P13B, P5C, using yarn B, inc in last st. 41 sts.
Cont in this way until 50th row of chart 1 has been worked (change to 3¼mm (US3) circular needle and work in rows when there are sufficient sts). 185 sts.
Shape armholes
Keep chart correct.
51st row Using yarn J, K2 tog, work 90 sts from chart, M1 in yarn J, K1J (centre st), M1 in yarn J, work 90 sts from chart, using yarn J, K2 tog.
52nd row Keeping chart correct, P to end. 185 sts.
Cont in this way until 110th row of chart has been worked.
Shape body
Cont working as set from chart, *at the same time* cast on 8 sts at beg of next 2 rows. 201 sts.
Now cont as set until 160th row of chart has been worked.
Divide for side insets
161st row Using yarn J, K2 tog, K98, M1 and turn leaving rem sts on a spare needle. 100 sts.
** Now commence rib and st st colour patt from chart 2, noting to work rs rows from right to left and ws rows from left to right.
Beg with a ws row, P 1 row, then dec 1 st at each end of every row until 2 sts rem. Work 2 tog and fasten off.
With rs of work facing return to sts on spare needle, rejoin J, K centre st, then K to last 2 sts, K2 tog. 100 sts.
Complete as for first side from ** to end.

FRONT
Work as given for back

This is quite an ambitious sweater and definitely not for a beginner, as very careful following of charts is essential to work the pattern successfully.

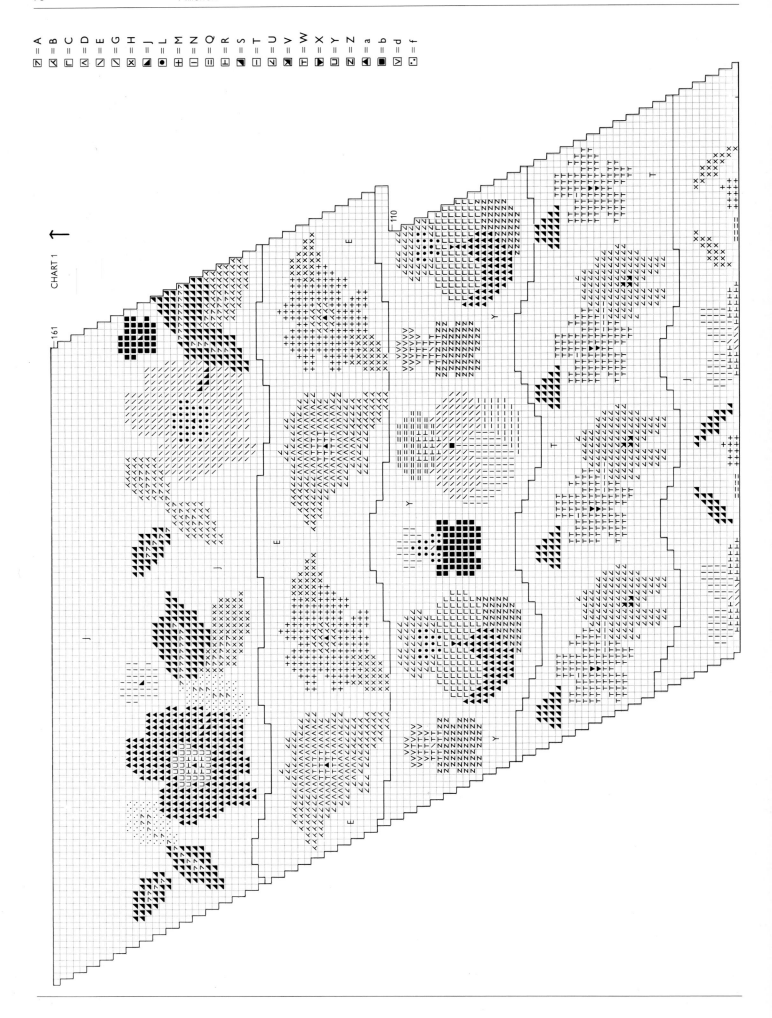

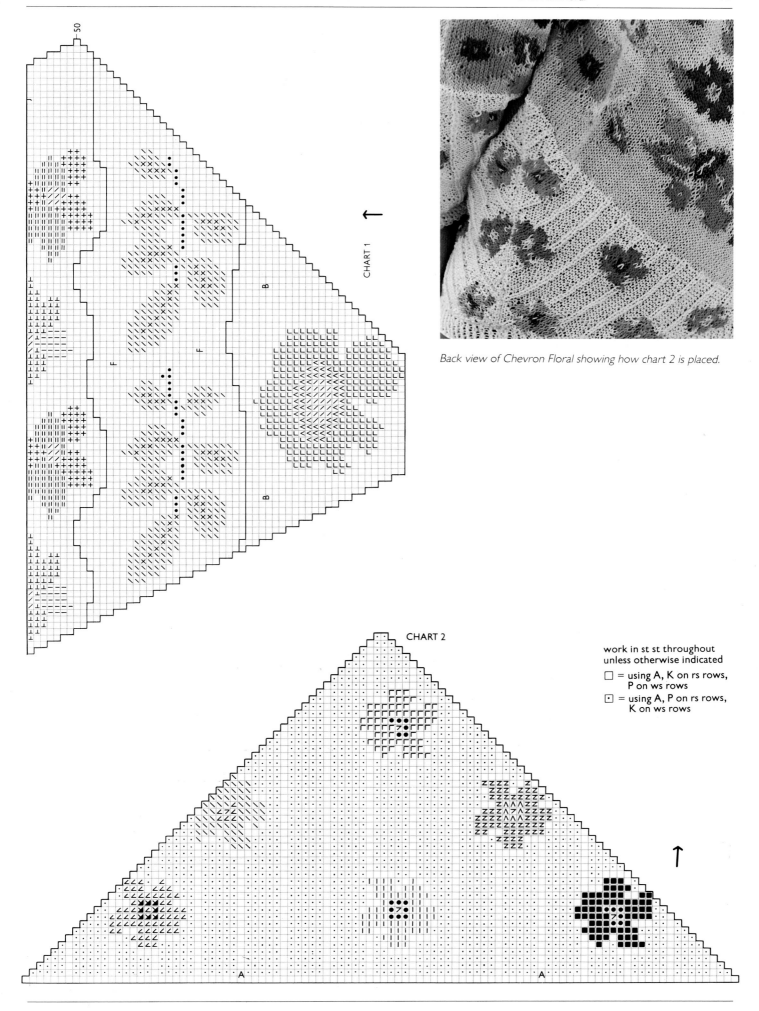

Back view of Chevron Floral showing how chart 2 is placed.

CHART 1

CHART 2

work in st st throughout
unless otherwise indicated

☐ = using A, K on rs rows,
P on ws rows

⊡ = using A, P on rs rows,
K on ws rows

SLEEVES

Using 3mm (US2) needles and yarn A, cast on 64 sts and work 8 rows K1, P1 rib.
Change to 3¼mm (US3) needles and commence rib and st st colour patt from chart 3, inc and work into patt 1 st at each end of every foll 4th row until there are 138 sts.
Cont straight until 164th row of chart has been worked.
Cast off.

BACK YOKE

With rs of work facing, using 3mm (US2) needles and yarn A, K up 128 sts evenly along cast-on edge of back.
Work in K1 tbl, P1 rib until work measures 25cm (9¾in) from cast-on sts for armhole.
Cast off in rib.

FRONT YOKE

With rs of work facing, using 3mm (US2) needles and yarn A, K up 128 sts evenly along cast-on edge of front.
Work 5 rows K1 tbl, P1 rib.
Shape neck
Next row Rib 44, and turn, leaving rem sts on a spare needle.
Cast off 2 sts at beg of next and every foll alt row until 34 sts rem. Work straight until front matches back to cast-off edge.
Cast off in rib. With rs of work facing, return to sts on spare needle, rejoin yarn A, cast off centre 40 sts, rib to end. Work 1 row.
Complete as given for first side of neck.

LOWER HEMS (back and front alike)

With rs of work facing, using 3mm (US2) needles and yarn A, K up 140 sts evenly across lower edge.
Work 8 rows K1 tbl, P1 rib.
Cast off in rib.

NECK EDGING

Join right shoulder seam.
With rs of work facing, using 2.50mm (USC) crochet hook and yarn A, work crochet picot edging as foll:
1st row Work in double crochet around neck edge.
2nd row *1 double crochet into each of next 3 double crochet, 4 chain, slip st into last double crochet; rep from *.

TO MAKE UP

Join left shoulder seam.
Set in sleeves, joining cast-off sts at underarm to final rows of sleeve. Join side and sleeve seams.

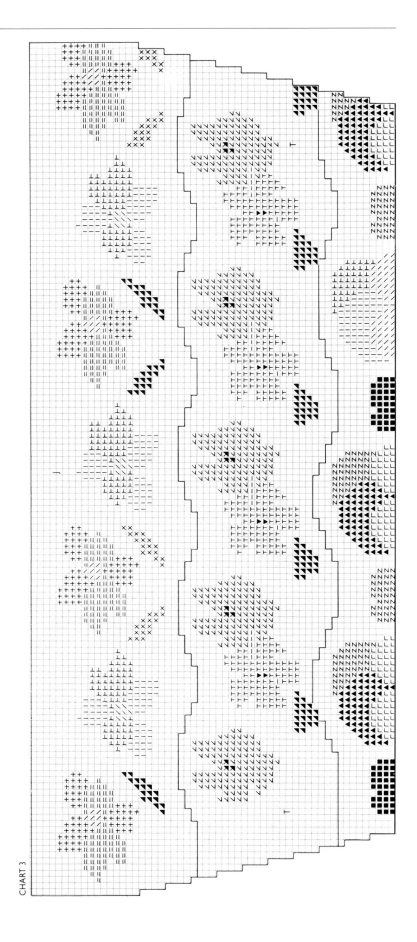

CHART 3

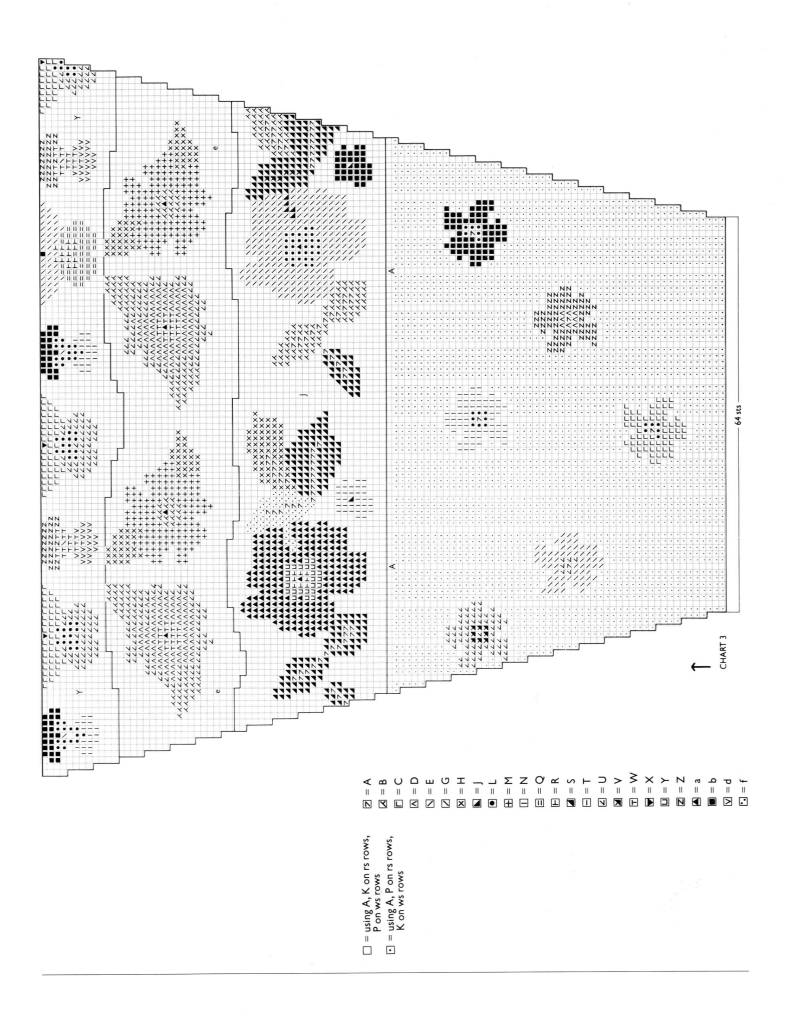

64 sts

CHART 3

☐ = A
☒ = B
☐ = C
☐ = D
☐ = E
☐ = G
☒ = H
☐ = J
☐ = L
☐ = M
☐ = N
☐ = Q
☐ = R
☐ = S
☐ = T
☐ = U
☐ = V
☐ = W
☐ = X
☐ = Y
☐ = Z
☐ = a
☐ = b
☐ = d
☐ = f

☐ = using A, K on rs rows,
     P on ws rows

☐ = using A, P on rs rows,
     K on ws rows

Flower Vases

This theme of pots, vases or baskets filled with flowers is one I've returned to from time to time, and it continues to intrigue me. The vases are each worked in a different stitch pattern, which adds a certain richness of texture.

SIZE
To fit one size only up to 96cm (38in) bust
Actual width measurement 107cm (42in)
Length to shoulder 63cm (24¾in)
Sleeve seam 48.5cm (19in)

MATERIALS
450g (18oz) 4-ply in main colour (A)
50g (2oz) in 1 contrast colour (Y)
25g (1oz) in each of 24 contrast colours
    (B, C, D, E, F, G, H, J, L, M, N, Q, R, S, T, U, V,
    W, X, Z, a, b, d, e)
1 pair each 3mm (US2) and 3¼mm (US3) needles
Cable needle

TENSION
28 sts and 35 rows to 10cm (4in) over colour patt
on 3¼mm (US3) needles.

SPECIAL ABBREVIATIONS
T2bK – sl next st on to cable needle and hold at back, K1 then K1 from cable needle.
T2bP – sl next st on to cable needle and hold at back, K1 then P1 from cable needle.
T2fK – sl next st on to cable needle and hold at front, K1 then K1 from cable needle.
T2fP – sl next st on to cable needle and hold at front, K1 then P1 from cable needle.

SPECIAL INSTRUCTIONS
Blackberry stitch
1st row (ws) *P3 tog, (K1, P1, K1) into next st; rep from * to end.
2nd and 4th rows P.
3rd row *(K1, P1, K1) into next st, P3 tog; rep from * to end.
Rep these 4 rows.

With 25 colours and many textures to deal with, this is quite a challenging pattern, but you can make life easier, if you wish, by simply leaving out the random spots on the background.

Moss stitch
Worked over an even number of sts:
1st row (K1, P1).to end.
2nd row (P1, K1) to end.
Rep these 2 rows.
Worked over an odd number of sts:
All rows K1, (P1, K1) to end.

Basket stitch
1st row (rs) (P4, K4) to end.
2nd row (P4, K4) to end.
3rd-4th rows Rep 1st and 2nd rows again.
5th row (K4, P4) to end.
6th row (K4, P4) to end.
7th-8th rows Rep 5th and 6th rows again.
Rep these 8 rows.

Lattice panel
1st row (rs) (P3, T2bK, P3) twice.
2nd and foll alt rows K the P sts and P the K sts of previous row.
3rd row (P2, T2bP, T2fP, P2) twice.
5th row (P1, T2bP, P2, T2fP, P1) twice.
7th row (T2bP, P4, T2fP) twice.
9th row K1, P6, T2fK, P6, K1.
11th row (T2fP, P4, T2bP) twice.
13th row (P1, T2fP, P2, T2bP, P1) twice.
15th row (P2, T2fP, T2bP, P2) twice.
16th row As 2nd row.
These 16 rows form the panel.

BACK
Using 3mm (US2) needles and yarn A, cast on 150 sts. Work in K2, P2, rib as foll:
1st row (rs) K2, (P2, K2) to end.
2nd row P2, (K2, P2) to end.
Rep these 2 rows 7 times more.
Change to 3¼mm (US3) needles and commence texture and colour patt from chart 1; use separate lengths of yarn for each colour area and twist yarns tog at colour joins to avoid holes.
1st row (rs) K14A, work 1st row of chart 1, K8A.
2nd row P8A, work 2nd row of chart 1, P14A.
These 2 rows establish position of chart with st st edge sts. Cont as set, keeping chart correct until work measures 39cm (15¼in) from cast-on edge, ending with a ws row.
Shape armholes
Cast off 5 sts at beg of next 4 rows. 130 sts. **
Cont without shaping until 24cm (9½in) from beg of armhole shaping ending with a ws row and working in st st in yarn A when chart is completed.
Shape shoulders
Cont in yarn A only, cast off 12 sts at beg of next 6 rows. Cast off rem 58 sts.

FRONT
Work as given for back to **.
Cont without shaping until work measures 19cm (7½in) from beg of armhole shaping ending with a

CHART 1

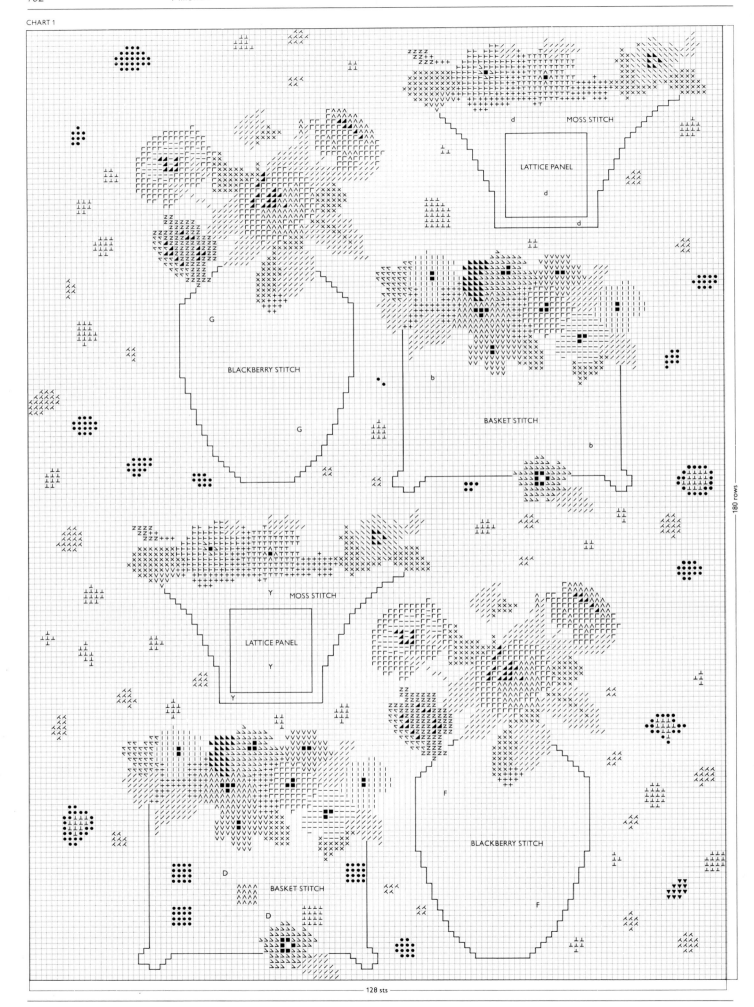

MOSS STITCH

LATTICE PANEL

BLACKBERRY STITCH

BASKET STITCH

MOSS STITCH

LATTICE PANEL

BLACKBERRY STITCH

BASKET STITCH

180 rows

128 sts

work in st st throughout
unless otherwise indicated

☐ = A
◪ = B
◪ = C
◼ = E
⊞ = G
⊡ = H
◪ = J
▼ = L
✕ = M
⊟ = N
☑ = Q
⊞ = R
▢ = S
◫ = T
◪ = U
◪ = V
◪ = W
◪ = X
◫ = Z
◪ = a
⊞ = b
◪ = e

ws row and working in st st in yarn A when chart is completed.

Shape neck
Next row Patt 50 sts, turn and leave rem sts on a spare needle.
Dec 1 st at neck edge on every row until 36 sts rem.
Cont without shaping, until work matches back to shoulder, ending at armhole edge.

Shape shoulder
Cast off 12 sts at beg of next and foll alt row.
Work 1 row.
Cast off rem 12 sts.
With rs of work facing, return to sts on spare needle, rejoin yarn, cast off centre 30 sts, patt to end.
Complete to match first side, reversing all shapings.

SLEEVES
Using 3mm (US2) needles and yarn A, cast on 60 sts and work 30 rows in K2, P2 rib.
Change to 3¼mm (US3) needles and cont working in colour patt from chart 2; work 1st–68th rows, then rep 31st–68th rows only, *at the same time* inc and work into st st and yarn A 1 st at each end of next and every foll 3rd row until there are 144 sts.
Now cont without further shaping until work measures 48.5cm (19in) from cast-on edge, ending with a ws row.

Shape top
Cast off 5 sts at beg of next 2 rows. Dec 1 st at each end of every row until 124 sts rem, ending with a ws row. Cast off.

NECKBAND
Join right shoulder seam.
With rs of work facing, using 3mm (US2) needles and yarn A, K up 26 sts down left side of neck, 30 sts across centre front, 26 sts up right side of neck and 58 sts across back neck. 140 sts.
Work 6 rows in K2, P2 rib.
Cast off in rib.

TO MAKE UP
Join left shoulder and neckband seams.
Set in sleeves. Join side and sleeve seams.

CHART 2

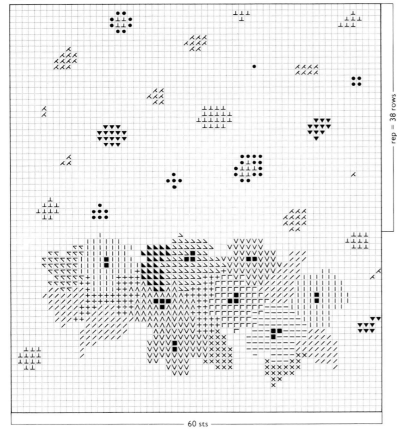

rep = 38 rows

60 sts

Patchwork

This simple cropped cardigan is worked in warm earthy colours in a chequered design of double-moss stitch squares and lots of small multi-coloured flowers. The version shown here is knitted in wool, but it would look equally good in cotton or silk yarns.

SIZE
To fit one size only up to 102cm (40in) bust
Actual width measurement 115cm (45¼in)
Llength to shoulder 58cm (22¾in)
Sleeve seam 49cm (19¼in)

MATERIALS
400g (8oz) 4-ply in main colour (A)
50g (2oz) in each of 12 contrast colours
  (C, D, E, G, H, M, N, R, T, V, X, a)
25g (1oz) in each of 12 contrast colours
  (B, F, J, L, Q, S, U, W, Y, Z, b, c)
1 pair each 3mm (US2) and 3¼mm (US3) needles
9 buttons

TENSION
27 sts and 36 rows to 10cm (4in) over chart 1
colour patt on 3¼mm (US3) needles.

BACK
Using 3mm (US2) needles and yarn A, cast on 156
sts.
Work 20 rows in K1, P1 rib.
Change to 3¼mm (US3) needles and commence
colour patt from chart 1; use separate lengths of
yarn for each colour area and twist yarns tog at
colour joins to avoid holes.
Cont until 114 rows have been worked from chart.
Shape armholes
Dec 1 st at each end of next 7 rows. 142 sts.
Cont without shaping until 196 rows have been
worked from chart, ending with a ws row.
Cast off.

LEFT FRONT
Using 3mm (US2) needles and yarn A, cast on 75
sts.
Cont in rib as folls:
1st row (rs) K1, (P1, K1) to end.
2nd row P1, (K1, P1) to end.
These 2 rows form the rib. Rep last 2 rows 9 times
more.
Change to 3¼mm (US3) needles and cont in colour
patt from chart 1 until 114 rows have been worked.
Shape armhole
Dec 1 st at armhole edge on next 7 rows. 68 sts.
Cont without shaping until 185 rows have been
worked from chart 1 ending with a rs row.
Shape neck
Keeping chart correct, cast off 12 sts at beg of next
row and 4 sts at beg of 4 foll alt rows. 40 sts.
Cont without shaping until 196 rows have been
worked from chart 1.
Cast off.

This little crew-necked cardigan has a certain old-fashioned innocence about it, reminiscent of the American New England style.

CHART 1

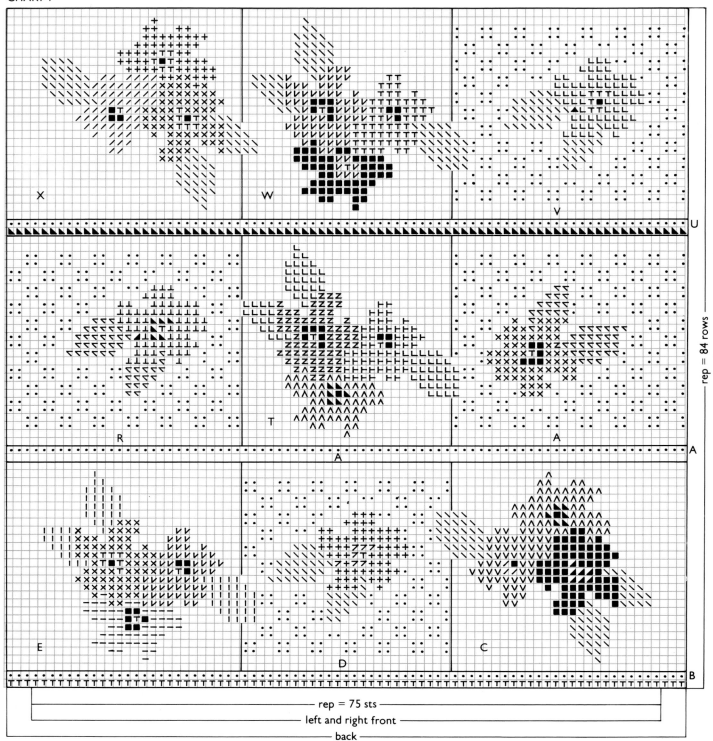

rep = 84 rows

rep = 75 sts
left and right front
back

work.in st st unless
otherwise indicated

☐ = K on rs rows,
P on ws rows
⊡ = P on rs rows,
K on ws rows

⧄ = A	⊠ = M	⊙ = X
⊤ = B	�inverted V = N	⊿ = Y
⊿ = D	⊞ = Q	⊔ = Z
⊟ = F	◩ = R	⊞ = a
◩ = G	⋀ = S	⌐ = b
■ = H	⊓ = T	⊿ = c
⊓ = J	◣ = U	
⊿ = L	▲ = V	

CHART 2

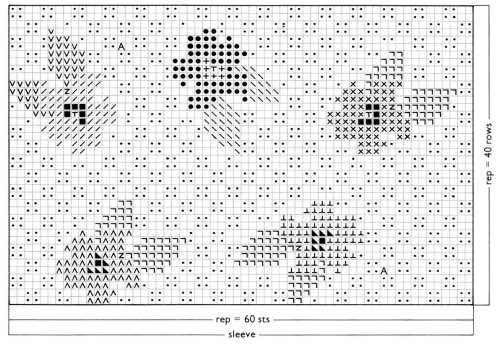

rep = 40 rows

rep = 60 sts

sleeve

RIGHT FRONT

Work as given for left front, reversing shapings by working 1 row more before armhole and neck shaping.

SLEEVES

Using 3mm (US2) needles and yarn c, cast on 60 sts.
Work 16 rows in K1, P1 rib.
Change to yarn A and work a further 42 rows in rib.
Change to 3¼mm (US3) needles and work in double moss st as foll:
1st row (rs) (P2, K2) to end.
2nd row As 1st row.
3rd row (K2, P2) to end.
4th row As 3rd row.
Now cont in colour patt from chart 2, *at the same time* inc and work into patt 1 st at each end of every 3rd row until there are 140 sts.
Now cont without further shaping until 138 rows have been worked from chart 2.
Cast off.

BUTTON BAND

Using 3mm (US2) needles and yarn A, cast on 11 sts.
Work in K1, P1 rib as given for left front until band when slightly stretched, fits up right front to neck edge, ending with a ws row.
Do not cut yarn.
Leave sts on a holder.
Place 9 button markers on button band, the first marker 7 rows from cast-on edge, and the last marker 2 rows from cast-off edge, with rem 7 evenly spaced between.

BUTTONHOLE BAND

Work as given for button band but cut yarn and leave sts on a holder and make buttonholes as markers are reached as foll:
1st buttonhole row Rib 4, cast off 3 sts, rib to end of row.
2nd buttonhole row Rib to end, casting on 3 sts over those cast off in previous row.

NECKBAND

Join shoulder seams.
Sew on button and buttonhole bands. With rs of work facing, using 3mm (US2) needles and yarn A, rib 11 sts from button band, K up 29 sts up right front neck, 53 sts across back neck, 29 sts down left front neck and rib across 11 sts from buttonhole band. 133 sts.
Beg with a 2nd row, work 8 rows in K1, P1 rib as given for left front. Cast off in rib.

TO MAKE UP

Set in sleeves. Join side and sleeve seams.
Sew on buttons.

Leaves and Berries

Tapestry

The richly textured patterns on the fronts of this design may look daunting, but the back, at least, is plain sailing – one colour only in alternating blocks of moss stitch and stocking stitch.

SIZE
To fit one size only up to 97cm (38in) bust
Actual width measurement 102cm (40in)
Length to shoulder 62cm (24¼in)
Sleeve seam 51cm (20in)

MATERIALS
650g (26oz) 4-ply in main colour (A)
25g (1oz) in each of 21 contrast colours
   (B, C, D, E, F, G, H, J, L, M, N, Q, R, S, T, U, V, W, X, Y, Z)
1 pair each 2¼mm (US2) and 3¼mm (US3) needles
9 buttons

TENSION
28 sts and 50 rows to 10cm (4in) over moss st on 3¼mm (US3) needles.

SPECIAL INSTRUCTIONS

Moss stitch
Worked over an even number of sts:
1st row (K1, P1) to end.
2nd row (P1, K1) to end.
Rep these 2 rows.
Worked over an odd number of sts:
All rows K1, (P1, K1) to end.

Make bobbles
1st row (rs) Using yarn specified, (K1, P1, K1, P1, K1) into next st, turn, K5, turn, P5, turn, K5, turn, P5 tog.
2nd row (ws) Work into back of bobble st.

BACK
Using 2¾mm (US2) needles and yarn A, cast on 140 sts.
Work 14 rows in K1 tbl, P1 rib.
Change to 3¼mm (US3) needles and cont in st st and moss st block patt.
1st row (rs) K2, (moss st 8, K8) to last 10 sts, moss st 8, K2.
2nd row P2, (moss st 8, P8) to last 10 sts, moss st 8, P2.
3rd-8th rows Rep 1st and 2nd rows 3 times more.
9th row Moss st 2, (K8, moss st 8) to last 10 sts, K8, moss st 2.
10th row Moss st 2, (P8, moss st 8) to last 10 sts, P8, moss st 2.
11th-16th rows Rep 9th and 10th rows 3 times more.
These 16 rows form the block patt.
Cont in patt until work measures 39.5cm (15½in) from cast-on edge, ending with a ws row.
Shape armholes
Cast off 7 sts at beg of next 2 rows. 126 sts.
Now work straight until back measures 22.5cm (8¾in) from beg of armhole shaping, ending with a ws row.
Shape shoulders
Cast off 14 sts at beg of next 4 rows and 13 sts at beg of foll 2 rows.
Cast off rem 44 sts.

RIGHT FRONT
Using 2¾mm (US2) needles and yarn A, cast on 70 sts. Work 14 rows K1 tbl, P1 rib.
Change to 3¼mm (US3) needles and work in colour patt from chart, working in st st unless otherwise indicated; use separate lengths of yarn for each colour area and twist yarns tog at colour joins to avoid holes.
1st row (rs) Work 1st row of chart, using yarn A, moss st 8.
2nd row Using yarn A, moss st 8, work 2nd row of chart.
These 2 rows establish the position of chart with moss st at side edge.
Keeping chart correct, cont until work matches back to armhole, ending at side edge.
Shape armhole
Cast off 7 sts at beg of next row. 63 sts.
Keeping patt correct, cont until work measures 15.5cm (6in) from beg of armhole shaping, ending at front edge, *at the same time* when 212 rows have been worked from chart, cont in yarn A and st st only.
Shape neck
Cast off 12 sts at beg of next row and 2 sts at beg of every foll alt row until 41 sts rem.
Cont straight until front matches back to shoulder shaping, ending at armhole edge.
Shape shoulder
Cast off 14 sts at beg of next and foll alt row.
Work 1 row. Cast off rem 13 sts.

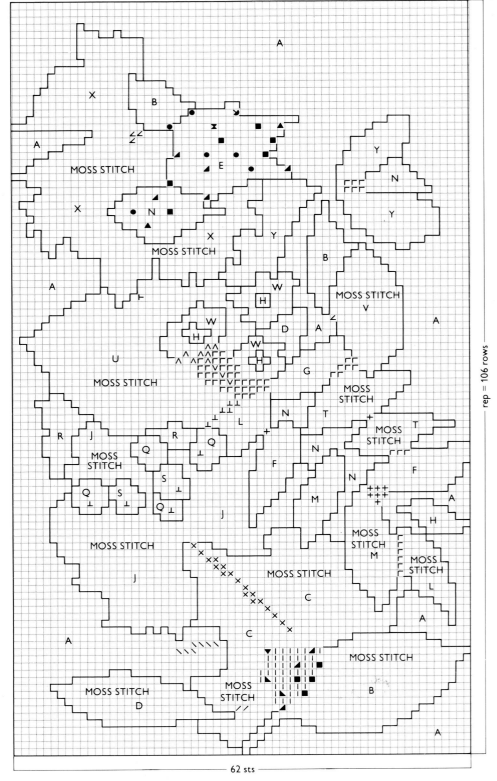

rep = 106 rows

62 sts

LEFT FRONT

Work as given for right front, reversing all shapings and placing chart as foll:
1st row (rs) Using yarn A, moss st 8, work 1st row of chart.
2nd row Work 2nd row of chart, using yarn A, moss st 8.

SLEEVES

Using 2¾mm (US2) and yarn A, cast on 56 sts.
Work 10cm (4in) in K1 tbl, P1 rib, ending with a ws row.
Change to 3¼mm (US3) needles and beg with a K row, work 4 rows st st.

Next row K6A, make bobble in yarn G, K6A, make bobble in yarn C, K6A, make bobble in yarn M, K6A, make bobble in yarn F, K6A, make bobble in yarn D, K6A, make bobble in yarn L, K6A, make bobble in yarn M, K7A.
Next row Using yarn A, P7, (P1 tbl, P6) to end.
Now cont in moss st, inc and work into moss st 1 st at each end of next and every foll 4th row until there are 140 sts. Cont straight until work measures 51cm (20in) from beg, ending with a ws row.
Shape top
Cast off 5 sts at beg of next 2 rows and 3 sts at beg of foll 2 rows.
Cast off rem 124 sts.

□ = A
◩ = B
◪ = C
◨ = D
▯ = E
☒ = J
⊞ = N
⊡ = R
▽ = U
△ = V
⊟ = X

● = make bobble in C
◣ = make bobble in D
■ = make bobble in F
◪ = make bobble in G
▼ = make bobble in H
✖ = make bobble in L
▲ = make bobble in M
◩ = make bobble in Z

BUTTONHOLE BAND
Work as given for button band, *at the same time* making buttonholes opposite button markers as foll:
1st buttonhole row (rs) Moss st 4, cast off 3 sts, moss st to end.
2nd buttonhole row Moss st to end, casting on 3 sts over those cast off in previous row.

COLLAR
Join shoulder seams.
Sew on front bands.
Using 2¾mm (US2) needles and yarn A, cast on 22 sts. Work 4 rows K1 tbl, P1 rib.
** **Next row** K4A, make bobble in yarn C, K5A, make bobble in yarn F, K5A, make bobble in yarn D, K5A.
Next row Using yarn A, P5, (P1 tbl, P5) twice, P1 tbl, P4. **
Now cont in moss st and yarn A until collar is long enough, when slightly stretched, to fit from the outer edge of buttonhole band, around neck edge to centre of button band, ending with a ws row.
Work as given from ** to ** again, but using yarn F instead of C, yarn D instead of F and yarn M instead of D.
Cont in yarn A and work 4 rows K1 tbl, P1 rib.
Cast off in rib.

TO MAKE UP
Set in sleeves, sewing top around entire armhole edge. Join side and sleeve seams.
Beg and ending at outer edges of front bands, sew on collar.
Sew on buttons.

BUTTON BAND
Using 2¾mm (US2) needles and yarn A, cast on 11 sts.
Cont in moss st until band, when slightly stretched, fits up front edge to beg of neck shaping, ending with a ws row.
Cast off in patt.
Place 9 button markers on band, one 2cm (¾in) from cast-on edge and one 4cm (1½in) below beg of neck shaping, and the rest spaced evenly between.

Rowan Berries

Although you would never find a rowan tree climbing up a formal trellis like this, I like the way my version weaves in and out of the grid among the clusters of berries in shades of russet reds.

SIZE
To fit one size only up to 102cm (40in) bust
Actual width measurement 117cm (46in)
Length to shoulder 66cm (26in)
Sleeve seam 49.5cm (19½in)

MATERIALS
275g (11oz) 4-ply in main colour (A)
100g (4oz) in each of 4 contrast colours
   (B, E, G, H)
50g (2oz) in each of 6 contrast colours
   (C, D, F, J, L, M)
1 pair 3mm (US2) and 3¼mm (US3) needles

TENSION
28 sts and 34 rows to 10cm (4in) over chart patt
on 3¼mm (US3) needles

SPECIAL INSTRUCTIONS
To make bobbles
1st row (rs) Using yarn specified, (K1, P1, K1, P1, K1) into next st, turn, K5, turn, P5, turn, K5, turn, P5 tog.
2nd row (ws) Work into back of bobble st.

BACK
Using 3mm (US2) needles and yarn A, cast on 164 sts. Work 14 rows K1, P1 rib.
Change to 3¼mm (US3) needles and cont in st st colour patt from chart; use separate lengths of yarn for each colour area and twist yarns when changing colour to avoid a hole.
Work 1-56th rows of chart, then rep 9th-56th rows twice more. Now work 9th-60th rows.
Now cont in yarn A. ** Work 6 rows st st.
Shape shoulders
Cast off 15 sts at beg of next 6 rows.
Cast off rem 74 sts.

FRONT
Work as given for back to **.
Divide for neck
Next row K66 sts and turn, leaving rem sts on a spare needle.
Cast off 7 sts at beg of next and 2 foll alt rows, ending at armhole edge. 45 sts.
Shape shoulder
Cast off 15 sts at beg of next and foll alt row.
Work 1 row. Cast off rem 15 sts.
With rs of work facing, return to sts on spare needle, rejoin yarn, cast off centre 32 sts, K to end. 66 sts. Work 1 row.
Complete as given for first side of neck.

You have to like doing bobbles to make this sweater as there are probably hundreds of them, but without them the design completely loses its impact.

SLEEVES

Using 3mm (US2) needles and yarn A, cast on 60 sts.
Work 8cm (3 in) in K1, P1 rib, ending with a rs row.
Inc row Rib 5, (inc in next st, rib 9) 5 times, inc in next st, rib 4. 66 sts.
Change to 3¼mm (US3) needles and beg with a K row, cont in st st, inc 1 st at each end of next and every foll alt row until there are 102 sts.
Work 1 row.
Now cont in colour patt from chart, work 1st-56th rows, 9th-60th rows, then work 2 rows in yarn A only, *at the same time* inc and work into rem chart patt 1 st at each end of next and every foll 4th row until there are 108 sts.
Now cont to inc as before until there are 140 sts, but work extra sts into st st and yarn A only.
Cast off.

NECKBAND

Join right shoulder seam.
With rs of work facing, using 3mm (US2) needles and yarn A, K up 20 sts evenly down left side of neck, 32 sts from centre front, 20 st up right side of neck and 74 sts across back neck. 146 sts. Work 6 rows in K1, P1 rib.
Cast off in rib.

TO MAKE UP

Join left shoulder and neckband seam.
Sew in sleeves, placing centre of cast-off edge to shoulder seam.
Join side and sleeve seams.

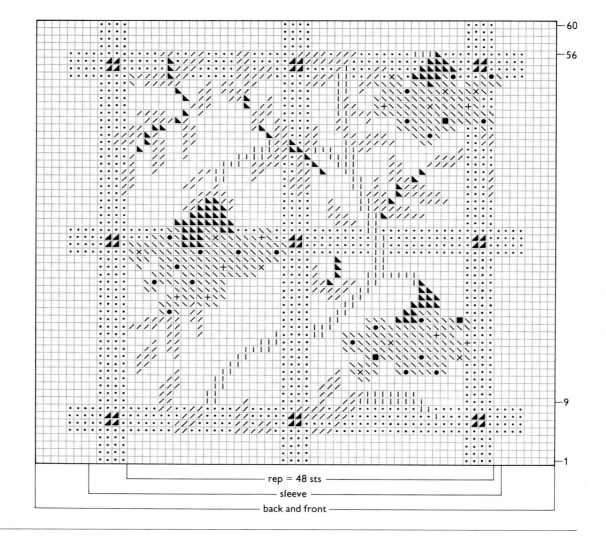

□ = A
⊡ = B
☑ = C
◪ = D
⑴ = E
◩ = F
⊡ = make bobble in G
☒ = make bobble in H
◼ = make bobble in J
⊞ = make bobble in L
◣ = M

rep = 48 sts
sleeve
back and front

Ivy Leaves

I wanted to do something with the classic guernsey shape so, to the traditional single-colour cabled pattern, I've added colour in the form of panels of twining ivy leaves between the swinging cables.

Providing you can cope with cables this is one of the easiest sweaters in the book to knit – only 8 colours.

CHART 1

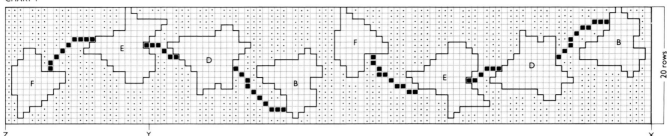

Z   Y   X   20 rows

CHART 2

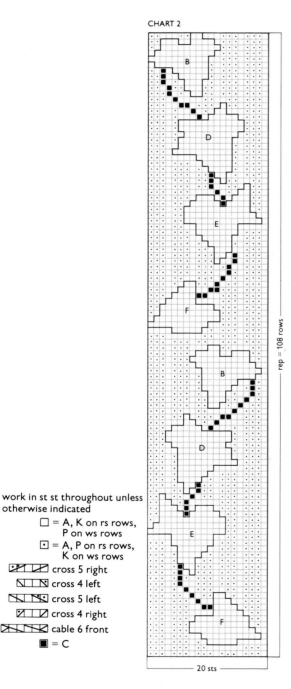

rep = 108 rows

20 sts

work in st st throughout unless otherwise indicated

□ = A, K on rs rows, P on ws rows

⊡ = A, P on rs rows, K on ws rows

cross 5 right

cross 4 left

cross 5 left

cross 4 right

cable 6 front

■ = C

CHART 3

rep = 28 rows

16 sts

SIZE
To fit one size only up to 102cm (40in) chest
Actual width measurement 113cm (44½in)
Length to shoulder 71cm (28in)
Sleeve seam 51cm (20in)

MATERIALS
500g (20oz) 4-ply in main colour (A)
50g (2oz) in each of 4 contrast colours
 (C, F, G, H)
25g (1oz) in each of 3 contrast colours (B, D, E)
1 pair 3mm (US2) needles
Cable needle

TENSION
34 sts and 37 rows to 10cm (4in) over chart patts
on 3mm (US2) needles

SPECIAL INSTRUCTIONS
cross 4 left – sl 3 sts on to cable needle, hold at front, P1, K3 from cable needle
cross 4 right – sl 1 st on to cable needle, hold at back, K3, P1 from cable needle
cross 5 left – sl 3 sts on to cable needle, hold at front, P2, K3 from cable needle
cross 5 right – sl 2 sts on to cable needle, hold at back, K3, P2 from cable needle
cable 6 front – sl 3 sts on to cable needle, hold at front, K3, K3 from cable needle

POD PANEL
Worked over 1 st.
1st row (rs) K1 tbl.
2nd and every foll alt row P.
3rd–10th rows Rep 1st and 2nd rows 4 times more.
11th row (K1, P1, K1) all into st.
13th row K1, (K1, P1, K1) all into next st, K1.
15th and 17th rows K5.
19th row K1, sl 2, K1, p2sso, K1.
21st row Sl 2, K1, p2sso.
23rd–28th rows Rep 1st and 2nd rows 3 times.
These 28 rows form the pod panel.

BACK
Using 3mm (US2) needles and yarn A, cast on 192 sts. Work 8 rows K1, P1 rib.
Commence rib and colour patt from chart 1; use separate lengths of yarn for each colour area, twisting yarns tog at colour joins to avoid holes. At side edges, work only complete leaf motifs and maintain rib instead.
1st row (rs) Work from X to Z, then from X to Y.
2nd row Work from Y to X, then from Z to X.
Cont in this way, work a further 18 rows.
Cont in A and K1, P3 rib.
Next row (K1, P3) to end.
Next row (K3, P1) to end.
Rep last 2 rows 7 times more.
Now cont in main patt.
1st row (rs) (Work 1st row of chart 2, P3A, work

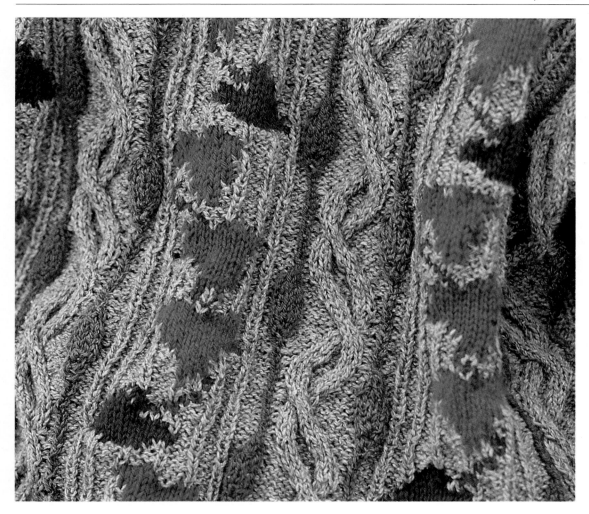

1st row of pod panel using yarn G, work 1st row of chart 3 using yarn A, work 15th row of pod panel using yarn H, P3A), 4 times.

2nd row (K3A, work 16th row of pod panel using yarn H, work 2nd row of chart 3 using yarn A, work 2nd row of pod panel using yarn G, K3A, work 2nd row of chart 2) 4 times.

These 2 rows establish the position of charts and pod panels and set the sts between.

Keeping all patts correct cont until work measures 71cm (28in) from cast-on edge, ending with a ws row.

Cast off

FRONT
Work as given for back until work measures 66cm (26in) from cast-on edge, ending with a ws row.

Divide for neck

Next row Patt 87 sts and turn leaving rem sts on a spare needle.

** Cast off 4 sts at beg of next and every foll alt row until 75 sts rem.

Cont straight until work measures 71cm (28in) from cast-on edge, ending with a ws row.

Cast off.

With rs of work facing return to sts on spare needle, rejoin yarn and cast off centre 18 sts, patt to end. 87 sts.

Work 1 row. Complete as given for first side of neck from ** to end.

SLEEVES
Using 3mm (US2) needles and yarn A, cast on 65 sts.

1st row (rs) K1, (P1, K1) to end.

2nd row P1, (K1, P1) to end.

Rep last 2 rows for 11cm (4¼in), end with rs row.

Inc row (Rib 4, inc in next st) 12 times, rib 5. 77 sts.

Commence patt.

1st row (rs) * P3A, work 1st row of pod panel using yarn G, work 1st row of chart 3 using yarn A, work 15th row of pod panel using yarn H, P3A *, work 1st row of chart 2, K1A, rep from * to * again.

2nd row * K3A, work 16th row of pod panel using yarn H, work 2nd row of chart 3 using yarn A, work 2nd row of pod panel using yarn G, K3A *, P1A, work 2nd row of chart 2, rep from * to * again.

These 2 rows establish the position of charts and pod panels and sets sts between.

Keeping all patts correct, cont to inc and work into P3, K1 rib 1 st at each end of next and every foll alt row until there are 191 sts.

Now cont straight until work measures 51cm (20in) from cast-on edge, ending with a ws row.

Cast off.

POLO COLLAR
Join right shoulder seam.

With rs of work facing, using 3mm (US2) needles and yarn A, K up 20 sts down left front neck, 30 sts from centre front, 20 sts up right side of neck and 60 sts across back neck. 130 sts.

Work 8cm (3in) in K1, P1 rib.

Cast off loosely in rib.

TO MAKE UP
Join left shoulder and collar seam, reversing half of the rib to fold back.

Set in sleeves placing centre of cast-off edge to shoulder seams. Join side and sleeve seams.

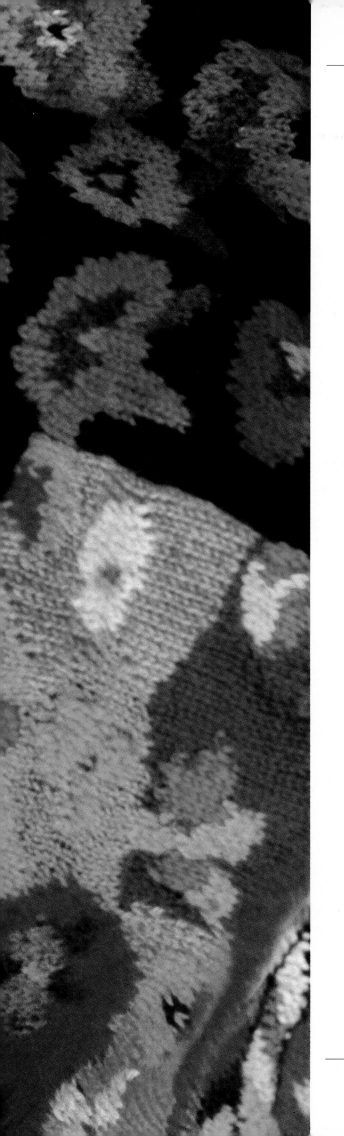

Flower Children

Flower Wheels

This little sweater with its cheerful stylized flower motif looks just as good on boys and girls. The matching hat, though, is probably better for a girl.

PULLOVER

SIZES

To fit 61[66:71]cm (24[26:28]in) chest
Actual width measurement 64[70:75.5] cm (25[27½:29¾in)
Length to shoulder 41[44:48]cm (16[17¼:19]in)
Sleeve seam 25[31.5:35]cm (9¾[12½:13¾]in)

MATERIALS

175[250,325]g (7[10,13]oz) 4-ply in main colour (A)
Oddments in each of 9 contrast colours
  (B, C, D, E, F, G, H, J, L)
1 pair each 3mm (US2) and 3¼ (US3) needles
3 buttons

TENSION

28 sts and 36 rows to 10cm (4in) over chart patt on 3¼mm (US3) needles

BACK

Using 3mm (US2) needles and yarn A, cast on 90[98:106] sts. Cont in K2, P2 rib:
1st row (rs) K2, (P2, K2) to end.
2nd row P2, (K2, P2) to end.
Rep last 2 rows for 5cm (2in), ending with a ws row.
Change to 3¼mm (US3) needles.
Now commence colour patt from chart on page 129, using separate lengths of yarn for each colour area and twist yarns tog at colour joins to avoid holes.
1st row (rs) K0[4:8]A, work 1st row of chart, K0[4:8]A.
2nd row P0[4:8]A, work 2nd row of chart, P0[4:8]A.
Cont in this way until work measures 24[26:29]cm (9½[10¼:11½]in) from cast-on edge, ending with a ws row.
Shape armholes
Cast off 5 sts at beg of next 2 rows. 80[88:96] sts.
**
Cont without shaping until work measures 41[44:48]cm (16[17¼:19]in) from cast-on edge working only complete wheel motifs, ending with a ws row.
Cast-off, marking centre 32[36:40] sts for back neck.

FRONT

Works as given for back to **.
Cont without shaping working only complete wheel motifs, until work measures 37[39.5:43]cm (14½[15½:17]in) from cast-on edge, ending with ws row.
Divide for neck
Keeping chart correct, patt 31[34:37] sts and turn, leaving rem sts on a spare needle.
*** Cast off 3[2:3] sts at beg on next row and 2 sts at beg of every foll alt row until 24[26:28] sts rem. ***
Cont straight until work measures 8 rows fewer than back, ending with a ws row.
Commence buttonhole band:
1st row K0[2:0], (P2, K2) to end.
2nd row (P2, K2) to last (0[2:0] sts, P0[2:0].
1st buttonhole row Rib 4[6:6], (cast off 3, rib 7[7:8]) twice.
2nd buttonhole row Rib to end, casting on 3 sts over those cast off in previous row.
Rib 3 more rows. Cast off in rib.
With rs of work facing, return to sts on spare needle, rejoin yarn, cast off centre 18[20:22] sts, patt to end.
Work 1 row, then work from *** to *** as given

for first side of neck.
Cont straight until work matches back to shoulder, ending with a ws row.
Cast off.

SLEEVES

Using 3mm (US2) needles and yarn A, cast on 42[46:50] sts and work 7cm (2¾in) in K2, P2 rib as given for back, ending with a rs row.
Inc row Rib 4[3:5], (inc in next st, rib 2) to last 5[4:6] sts, inc in next st, rib to end. 54[60:64] sts.
Change to 3¼mm (US3) needles.
Commence working in colour patt from chart on page 129.
1st row (rs) K0[3:5]A, work 1st row of chart, K0[3:5]A.
2nd row P0[3:5]A, work 2nd row of chart, P0[3:5]A.
Cont in this way, keeping chart correct and only working whole motifs, inc and work into yarn A 1 st at each end of next and every foll 3rd[4th:4th] row until there are 96[102:106] sts.
Now cont without further shaping until 72[96:96] rows have been worked from chart. Work 0[0:12] rows in yarn A. Cast off.

BUTTON BAND

With rs of work facing, using 3mm (US2) needles and yarn A, K up 24[26:28] sts from left back

The clove colourway of the Flower Wheels sweater and bonnet, and (below) the sweater in blue tweed in the larger size.

work in st st throughout

□ = A unless otherwise
       indicated
☑ = B
⊞ = C
⊞ = D
⊠ = E
■ = F
◩ = G
◉ = H
⊡ = J

shoulder. Work 7 rows rib as given for buttonhole band, omitting buttonholes.
Cast off in rib.

NECKBAND
Join right shoulder seam.
With rs of work facing, using 3mm (US2) needles and yarn A, K up 6 sts from edge of buttonhole band, 14[17:18] sts down left front neck, 22[24:26] sts across front neck, 14[17:18] sts up right front neck, 40[44:48] sts across back neck and 6 sts from button band. 102[114:122] sts.

Beg with a 2nd row, work 3 rows in K2, P2 rib as given for back.
1st buttonhole row Rib 2, cast off 3 sts, rib to end.
2nd buttonhole row Rib to end, casting on 3 sts over those cast off.
Rib 2 more rows. Cast off in rib.

TO MAKE UP
Overlap and sew ends of button and buttonhole bands at armhole edge. Set in sleeves, sewing final rows to cast-off sts at underarm. Join side and sleeve seam. Sew on buttons.

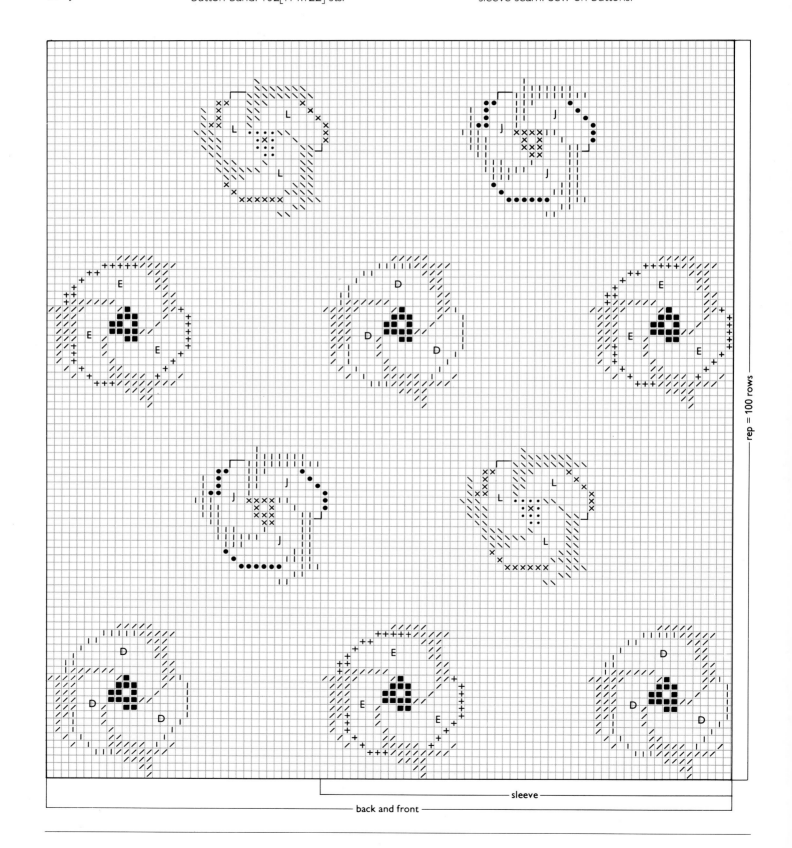

rep = 100 rows

— sleeve —

— back and front —

BONNET

SIZE
One size
Actual measurement around face 35cm (13¾in)

MATERIALS
50g (2oz) 4-ply in main colour (A)
Oddments in each of 8 contrast colours
 (B, C, D, E, F, G, H, J)
1 pair 2¾mm (US2) and 3mm (US2) needles

TENSION
28 sts and 36 rows to 10cm (4in) over chart patt
on 3mm (US2) needles

BONNET
Using 3mm (US2) needles and yarn G, cast on 98
sts.
** Beg with a P row, work 3 rows in st st.
Change to 2¾mm (US2) needles
Picot row K2, (yfwd, K2 tog) to end.
Change to 3mm (US2) needles.
Beg with P row, work 3 rows st st. **
Change to yarn A and work 6 rows st st.
Now commence colour st st patt from charts; use
separate lengths of yarn for each colour area and
twist yarns tog at colour joins to avoid holes.
1st row (rs) K10A, work 1st row of chart 1, K11A,
work 1st row of chart 2, K11A, work 1st row of
chart 3, K10A.
2nd row P10A, work 2nd row of chart 3, P11A,
work 2nd row of chart 2, P11A, work 2nd row of
chart 1, P10A.
These 2 rows set the position of charts with st st
between.
Work a further 19 rows.
Work 18 rows st st in yarn A.
Make picot tuck
Change to yarn B and work from ** to ** again.
Cont in yarn A.
Next row (K next st on needle tog with back of
loop of corresponding st in first row in yarn B) to
end.
Next row P.
Commence shaping back of head:
1st row (K8, K2 tog) to last 8 sts, K8. 89 sts.
2nd and every foll alt row P.
3rd row K6, K2 tog, (K7, K2 tog) to end. 79 sts.
5th row K5, K2 tog, (K6, K2 tog) to end. 69 sts.
7th row K4, K2 tog, (K5, K2 tog) to end. 59 sts.
Cont to dec 10 sts on every alt row as now set
until 29 sts rem, ending with a P row.
Next row K2, (K1, K2 tog) to end. 20 sts.
Cut yarn, thread through rem sts, draw up and
fasten off securely.

NECK EDGING
Join back seam.
Fold face edge hem to ws at picot row and
slipstitch in place.
With rs of work facing, using 3mm (US2) needles
and yarn A, K up 60 sts evenly around neck edge.
Work 6 rows K1, P1 rib.
Cast off in rib.

TO MAKE UP
Using 3 strands of yarn A tog, make two plaits each
46cm (18in) long and sew to neck edging for ties.
Make 2 tassels in yarn B and securely attach to
ends of ties.

The Flower Wheels bonnet.

CHART 1

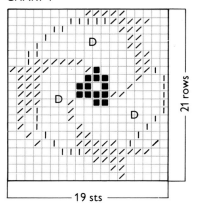

21 rows

19 sts

work in st st throughout

☐ = A unless otherwise
                indicated
☑ = B
Ⅱ = C
⊞ = D
☒ = E
■ = F
◨ = G
⊡ = H

CHART 2

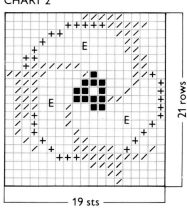

21 rows

19 sts

CHART 3

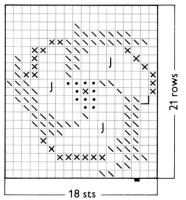

21 rows

18 sts

Rose Trellis

I once saw a half-finished pencil drawing of a trellis with roses which sparked off this fairly simple pullover. Probably because of the indigo blue and sugary colouring, it turned out to have an oriental feel.

SIZES
To fit 66-71[76-81]cm (26-28[30-32]in) chest
Actual width measurement 78[88] cm (30¾[34½]in)
Length to shoulder 49.5[53]cm (19½[21]in)
Sleeve seam 36[40]cm (14[15¾]in)

MATERIALS
300[350]g (12[12, 14]oz) 4-ply in main colour (A)
50g (2oz) in each of 3 contrast colours (B, G, H)
25g (1oz) in each of 10 contrast colours
  (C, D, E, F, J, L, M, N, Q, R)
1 pair each 3mm (US2) and 3¼ (US3) needles
2 buttons

TENSION
28.5 sts and 35 rows to 10cm (4in) over chart patt on 3¼mm (US3) needles.

BACK
Using 3mm (US2) needles and yarn A, cast on 112[126] sts.
Work in K1, P1 rib for 5cm (2in), ending with a ws row.
Change to 3¼mm (US3) needles.
Now commence colour patt from chart; work in st st throughout and use separate lengths of yarn for each colour area and twist yarns tog at colour joins to avoid holes.
1st row (rs) K2[9]A, work 1st row of chart, then K2[9]A.
2nd row P2[9]A, work 2nd row of chart, then P2[9]A.
Cont in this way keeping chart correct, work 3rd-52nd rows, 5th-52nd rows, then 5th-60th rows, ending with a ws row.
Cont in yarn A only.
Work 0[14] rows.

(Opposite) The Rose Trellis sweater (right) has an interesting side-opening collar. The other sweater (left) is a woollen version of the Chevron Floral design on page 94.

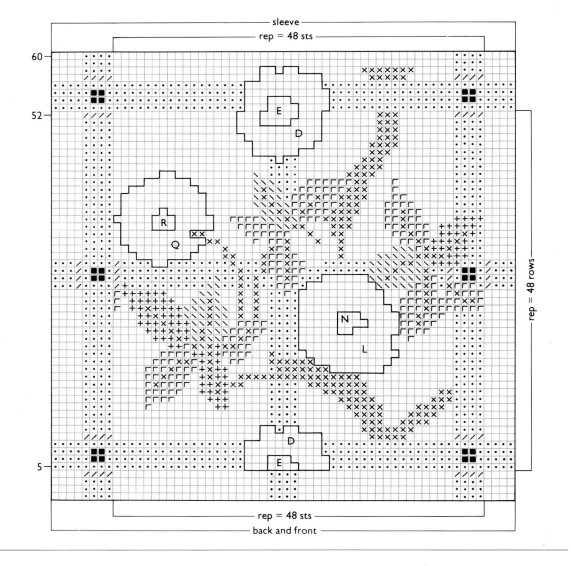

work in st st throughout

☐ = A unless otherwise
        indicated
• = B
◨ = C
■ = F
☒ = G
⊞ = H
⌐ = J
◹ = M

Shape shoulders
Cast off 12 sts at beg of next 2 rows. and 9[11] sts at beg of foll 4 rows.
Cast of rem 52[58] sts.

FRONT
Works as given for back until work measures 14 rows fewer than back to shoulder shaping, ending with a ws row.
Divide for neck
Next row Cont as for back, work 44[48] sts and turn, leaving rem sts on a spare needle.
Cast off 2 sts at beg of next and every foll alt row until 30[34] sts rem, ending at armhole edge.
Shape shoulder
Cast off 12 sts at beg of next row and 9[11] sts at beg of foll row.
Work 1 row.
Cast off rem 9[11] sts.
With rs of work facing, return to sts on spare needle, rejoin yarn, cast off centre 24[30] sts, patt to end.
Work 1 row, then work as given for first side of neck.

SLEEVES
Using 3¼mm (US3) needles and yarn A, cast on 112[126] sts and work 0[4] rows st st.
Now turn chart upside down and commence working in colour patt.
1st row (rs) K2[9]A, work 60th row of chart, K2[9]A.
2nd row P2[9]A, work 59th row of chart, P2[9]A.
Cont in this way keeping chart correct, work 58th-5th rows, 52nd-1st rows, then work 0[2] rows in yarn A only, and cont in K1, P1 rib *at the same time* dec 1 st at each end of next and every foll 4th row until 52[56] sts rem.

Now cont without further shaping until work measures 41[47]cm (16[18½]in) from cast-on edge, ending with a ws row.
Cast off in rib.

COLLAR
Using 3mm (US2) needles and yarn A, cast on 104[126] sts.
Next row (K1, P1) to end.
Rep last row 25[33] times more.
Cast off in patt.

BUTTONHOLE BAND
With rs of work facing, using 3mm (US2) needles and yarn A, K up 22[28] sts evenly along row ends of collar front.
Work 1 row in K1, P1 rib.
1st buttonhole row (Rib 6[9], cast off 3 sts) twice, rib to end.
2nd buttonhole row Rib to end, casting on 3 sts over those cast off.
Rib 1 more row.
Cast off in rib.

BUTTON BAND
Work to match buttonhole band, omitting buttonholes.

TO MAKE UP
Join shoulder seams.
Beginning and ending at left shoulder, sew collar to neck edges, overlapping ends of button and buttonhole bands.
Set in sleeves, placing centre of cast-off edge to shoulder seams.
Join side and sleeve seams, reversing for cuff to fold back.
Sew on buttons.

A detail of the Rose Trellis sweater.

Cloche

The leaf sprigs around this hat match a motif on the Chevron Floral design on page 94.
Worked on two needles, it is very easy and quick to make.

SIZE
One size
Actual measurement around face 56cm (22in)

MATERIALS
50g (2oz) 4-ply in main colour (A)
25g (1oz) in each of 5 contrast colours
   (B, C, D, E, F)
1 pair 3mm (US2) and 3¼mm (US3) and 3¾ (US4)
needles

TENSION
28 sts and 36 rows to 10cm (4in) over chart patt
on 3¼mm (US3) needles

HAT
Using 3mm (US2) needles and yarn A, cast on 156
sts.
Work 5cm (2in) in K1, P1 rib.
Now commence colour st st patt from chart; use
separate lengths of yarn for each colour area and
twist yarns tog at colour joins to avoid holes.
Work 20 rows of chart, then cont in yarn B only
and work 9 rows st. st.
Piping edge
Using a 3¾mm (US4) needle and yarn E, P 1 row
for foundation row.
Change to 3¼mm (US3) needles.
1st row (K3E, 1F), to end.
2nd row (P1F, 3E) to end.
3rd-7th rows Rep 1st and 2nd rows twice more,
then 1st row again.
8th row (Using yarn E, P next st on needle tog
with back of loop of corresponding st in foundation
row) to end.
Change to yarn F and commence crown:
Next row (K4, K2 tog) to end. 130 sts.
Beg P, work 5 rows st st.
Next row (K3, K2 tog) to end. 104 sts.
Beg P, work 5 rows st st.
Next row (K2, K2 tog) to end. 78 sts.
Change to yarn A.
Next row P2 tog, P to last 2 sts, P2 tog. 76 sts.
Beg K, work 4 rows st st.
Next row (K1, K2 tog) to last st, K1. 51 sts.
Next row K1, (P1, K1) to end.
Next row P1, (K1, P1) to end.
Rep last 2 rows twice more, then first of them
again.
Next row K1, (K2 tog) to end. 26 sts.
Next row (P2 tog) to end. 13 sts.
Cut yarn, thread through rem sts, draw up and
fasten off securely.

TO MAKE UP
Join back seam, reversing the seam for fold back
brim.

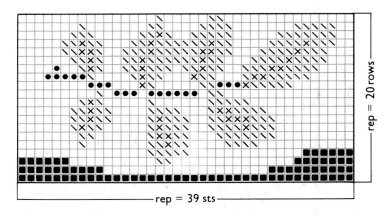

rep = 20 rows

rep = 39 sts

work in st st
throughout
■ = A   ◨ = C
□ = B   ☒ = D
                ◉ = E

Flower Tiles

This simple sweater lends itself to lots of different colourways, and you can use up all your oddments in it. It will be much more exciting to knit if you ignore my colours and just make up your own scheme. The helmet is given only for the smallest size.

This colourway uses many different shades of blue with flowers picked out in bright pinks.

work in st st
throughout
■ = A
☒ = J
☑ = L
☒ = J
⊞ = F

PULLOVER

SIZES
To fit 56[66:76]cm (22[26:30]in) chest
Actual width measurement 61[72:83]cm (24[28½:32½]in)
Length to shoulder 37[41:45.5]cm (14½[16:18]in)
Sleeve seam (cuff folded) 25.5[32:36.5]cm (10[12½:14½]in)

MATERIALS
100[125:125]g (4[5:5]oz) 4-ply in main colour (A)
Oddments in each of 14 contrast colours (B, C, D, E, F, G, H, J, L, M, N, Q , R, S)
1 pair each 3mm (US2) and 3¼ (US3) needles

TENSION
25 sts and 33 rows to 10cm (4in) over chart patt on 3¼mm (US3) needles

BACK
Using 3mm (US2) needles and yarn A, cast on 74[90:102] sts. Cont in K2, P2 rib:
1st row (rs) K2, (P2, K2) to end.
2nd row P2, (K2, P2) to end.
Rep last 2 rows for 5cm (2in), ending with a ws row, inc 1 st at each end last row on 1st and 3rd sizes only. 76[90:104] sts.
Change to 3¼mm (US3) needles. Now commence colour patt from chart; use separate lengths of yarn for each colour area and twist yarns tog at colour joins to avoid holes.
Work 56[60:70] rows, ending with a ws row.
Shape armholes
Cast off 5 sts at beg of next 2 rows. 66[80:90] sts.
**
Cont without shaping until 106[120:134] rows have been worked from chart, ending with a ws row.
Shape shoulders
Cast off 16[21:26] sts at beg of next 2 rows.
Cast off rem 34[38:42] sts.

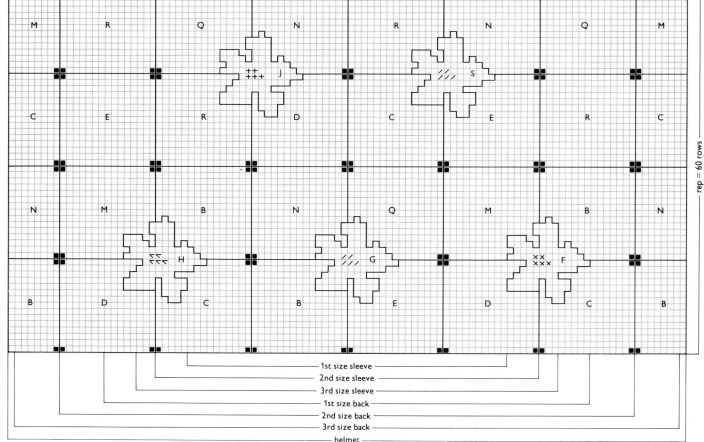

FRONT
Works as given for back to **.
Cont without shaping until work measures
10[10:16] rows fewer than back to shoulder
shaping, ending with a ws row.
Divide for neck
Keeping chart correct, patt 26[31:36] sts and turn,
leaving rem sts on a spare needle.
Cast off 2 sts at beg of next and every foll alt row
until 16[21:26] sts rem.
Work 0[0:6] rows straight, ending at armhole edge.
Shape shoulder
Cast off.
With rs of work facing, return to sts on spare
needle, rejoin yarn, cast off centre 14[18:22] sts,
patt to end.
Work 1 row, then work as given for first side of
neck.

SLEEVES
Using 3mm (US2) needles and yarn A, cast on
38[46:50] sts and work 5[7:7] cm (2[2¾:2¾in) in
K2, P2 rib as given for back, ending with a rs row.
Inc row Rib 2[3:2], (inc in next st, rib 2) to last
3[4:3] sts, inc in next st, rib to end. 50[60:66] sts.
Change to 3¼ (US3) needles.
Commence working in colour patt from chart.
Keeping chart correct, inc and work into patt 1 st at
each end of next and every foll 4th[5th:6th] row
until there are 78[90:96] sts.
Now cont without further shaping until 74[90:104]
rows have been worked from chart. Cast off.

COLLAR
Using 3mm (US2) needles and yarn A, cast on
88[98:123] sts.
1st row (rs) K3, (P2, K3) to end.
2nd row P3, (K2, P3) to end.
Commence two-colour rib, stranding contrast yarn
loosely across ws of work.
Next row KIA, KIM, KIA, (P2A, KIA, KIM, KIA)
to end.
Next row PIA, PIM, PIA, (K2A, PIA, PIM, PIA) to
end.
Rep last 2 rows until work measures 4[4:6]cm
(1½[1½:2½]in) from cast-on edge, ending with a ws
row.
Now cont in yarn A only and rep 1st and 2nd rows
twice more.
Cast off in rib.

FRONT EDGES (alike)
With rs of work facing, using 3mm (US2) needles
and yarn A, K up 14[14:20] sts along row ends of
collar.
Work 4 rows K1, P1 rib.
Cast off in rib.

TO MAKE UP
Join shoulder seam.
Set in sleeves, sewing final rows to cast-off sts at
underarm.
Join side and sleeve seams.
Sew on collar, beginning and ending at centre front
neck.

Here there is a mixture of bright glowing reds through to deep clover, with the flowers in brilliant blue-greens.

HELMET

SIZE
One size
Actual measurement around face 42.5cm (16¾in)

MATERIALS
25g (1oz) 4-ply in main colour (A)
Oddments in each of 9 contrast colours
  (B, C, D, E, F, G, H, J, L)
1 pair 3mm (US2) and 3¼mm (US3) needles
3mm (USC) crochet hook

TENSION
25 sts and 33 rows to 10cm (4in) over chart patt
on 3¼mm (US2) needles

EAR FLAPS (make 2)
Using 3¼mm (US3) needles and yarn A, cast on 7
sts.
P 1 row.
Commence two-colour st st:
1st row (K1B, 1A) in first st, K1A, 1B, 2A, 1B, K2A in
last st. 9 sts.
2nd row (P1B, 1A) in first st, P1A, 1B, 2A, 1B, 2A,
(P1B, 1A) in last st. 11 sts.
These 2 rows establish the patt, cont in this way,
inc and work into patt 1 st at each end of every
row until there are 21 sts.
Work 12 rows straight.
Cut yarn and leave sts on a holder.

CROWN
Using 3¼mm (US3) needles and yarn A, cast on 16
sts, with ws facing, P across sts of one flap, cast on
32 sts, with ws facing, P across sts of second ear
flap, cast on 16 sts. 106 sts.
P 1 row.
Change to yarn B and P 2 rows.
Change to yarn A and P 1 row.
Now work from chart for pullover.
Work 28 rows.
Next row (K1B, K2 in yarn colour as set by
previous row) to last st, K1B.
Next row P to end in yarn colours as set.
Next row K to end in yarn B.
Now cont in yarn A. P 1 row.

Shape top
1st row (K10, K2 tog) to last 10 sts, K10.
2nd, 4th and 6th rows P.
3rd row (K9, K2 tog) to last 10 sts, K10.
5th row (K8, K2 tog) to end.
7th row (K2A, 3H, 2A, K2A tog) to end.
8th and 10th rows P to end in yarn colours as set.
9th row (K2A, 3H, 1A, K2A tog) to end.
Cont in yarn H only.
11th row (K5, K2 tog) to end.
12th and every foll alt row P.
13th row (K4, K2 tog) to end.
15th row (K3, K2 tog) to end.
17th row (K2, K2 tog) to end.
18th row P2, (P2 tog) to last 3 sts, P3.
Cut yarn, thread through rem sts, draw up and
fasten off securely.

EDGING
With rs of work facing, using 3mm (US2) needles
and yarn H, K up 16 sts to first ear flap, * 22 sts
down side to point of ear flap and 22 sts up other
side *, K up 32 sts across brow of crown, rep from
* to *, K up 16 sts to centre back. 152 sts.
Cast-off loosely K-wise.

TO MAKE UP
Join back seam.
Using 3 strands of yarn H and crochet hook, make
2 chains each 30cm (11¾ in) long and sew one to
each ear flap point for ties.
Make a small tassel in yarn H for the ends of each
tie and attach securely.

*The tiles are worked here
in sunny colours – custard
yellows, chromes, through
to peach and apricot, with
flowers worked in
lavender. The helmet
pattern is given for the
blue colourway, not
shown here.*

Reading the Patterns

The patterns in this book are written in a fairly standard form so they will, I hope, be perfectly comprehensible to all averagely competent knitters. Nevertheless there are a few points which may be worth emphasizing for less experienced knitters, or for those whose skills are, perhaps, a little rusty.

SIZES

Some of the patterns provide instructions for several sizes. The smallest size is given first with the larger sizes following in square brackets. When choosing which size to knit, look at the *actual* measurements as well as the *to fit* measurement. Many of the garments are generously sized and you may wish to choose a size which will give you a tighter fit (or, indeed, *vice versa*). The sizes are given in metric with non-metric equivalents in the following parentheses. When following measurements through a pattern, use metric *or* non-metric measurements consistently. Don't jump from one to the other.

MATERIALS

In the Materials section of each pattern the yarns are quoted as generic types of yarn, which means that, if you wish, you can use any suitable four-ply or double knitting or whatever *providing* it can be knitted up to the correct tension (this means that, to be on the safe side, you should make a tension check with one ball before buying enough yarn for the whole garment). Where generic yarns are quoted the quantities can only be approximate; much depends on the precise composition of the yarn used. We have tried to be generous with the yarn allocations, but if you don't mind having yarn left over, then buy a few extra balls. For those who wish to reproduce the designs in the colourways shown in the photographs the specific qualities and shades are given on page 140, although the availability of the precise colours cannot indefinitely be guaranteed. All the designs are available in kit form, and this will give you the best chance of the closest possible match to the original, as well as being a more economic way of buying the yarn. (for more information on how to obtain kits see page 139).

CHARTS

Many of the designs in this book are worked from charts which are drawn with symbols rather than colours. If you find it difficult to follow the design through the chart, it can be helpful to photocopy that page of the book and hand-colour it. Many copying machines will also enlarge the charts if you find the squares too small.

TENSION

It is essential to check your tension before beginning to knit up a design. If your tension is not accurate your sweater or cardigan will not be the right size and the yarn quantities may be inadequate. Remember that the needle size given is only a recommendation. Some knitters may have to adjust the size up or down to achieve the tension given in the pattern.

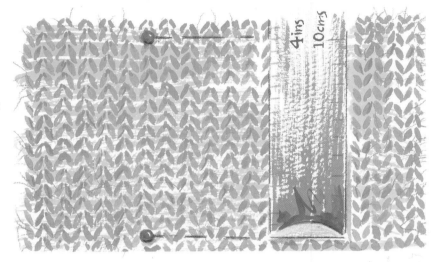

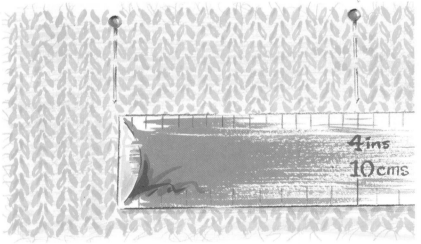

To check your tension knit up a sample using the yarn specified in the section and the stitch and needle size specified in the Tension section. (If it is a colour pattern, make sure you handle the yarn exactly as specified; this can make all the difference to the tension.) Then count the number of stitches and rows in your sample. If there are more stitches or rows to 10cm (4in) than there should be, your sample is too tight and you should knit up another one on larger needles. If there are fewer stitches or rows to 10cm (4in) than there should be, your sample is too loose and you should knit up another one using smaller needles. Keep on adjusting the needle size until the correct tension is obtained.

To measure row tension (top): place a ruler or tape measure alongside one column of stitches as shown. Insert a pin at the zero and 10cm (4in) marks. Count the stitches between tne pins.

To measure stitch tension (above): place a ruler or tape measure under one row of stitches. Insert a pin at the zero and 10cm (4in) marks. Count the stitches between the pins.

HANDLING YARNS

There are several methods which may be used to handle lots of different coloured yarns in multi-coloured patterns. They vary depending on the nature of the colour pattern – whether it is an all-over repeating pattern like Fair Isle, for example, or several separate motifs on a plain ground, and on whether the areas of colour are small or large, covering one or two stitches, or many. Fortunately you do not have to decide for yourself which method to use. The pattern will specify it and it is very important to use the method specified or the tension of the garment will be altered. The two commonest methods are Fair Isle and intarsia.

FAIR ISLE METHOD

The Fair Isle method is appropriate where only two or three colours are used in a row, and where the spans between the colours are short. The yarns not in use are either stranded (or 'floated') across the back of the work, or woven into each other in making the stitches. When stranding yarn, it is important to carry it very loosely across the back. If it is pulled too tightly the fabric will be puckered.

INTARSIA METHOD

The intarsia method is the one used in most of the patterns in this book. It is appropriate when many different colours are being used in a row, or when lots of separate motifs are being worked. By this method the yarns are twisted together at each colour join and then left in position to be worked on the next row.

When many different yarns are being used it can be difficult to avoid them becoming dreadfully tangled at the back of the work. If you use fairly generous lengths of yarn instead of balls, at least they can easily be pulled free of the tangle.

The Fair Isle method: (top) stranding in a knit row; (above) stranding in a purl row; (right) weaving yarns into the back of the work.

The intarsia method.

SWISS DARNING

Swiss darning is an embroidery stitch which exactly mimics the structure of knitted stocking stitch. It is a useful technique where small spots of colour are needed in a design. Instead of working them in with the rest of the knitting, Swiss-darn them on afterwards. Swiss darning can also be used to correct mistakes or to effect changes of mind about colours after the design is completed.

To work Swiss darning (right) use a yarn that is the same weight as the background fabric so that the stitches are evenly covered. Insert the needle through the base of the first stitch (a), then behind the base of the stitch above from b to c. Then take the needle back through the base of the first stitch (d) and out through the base of the second stitch to be covered (e).

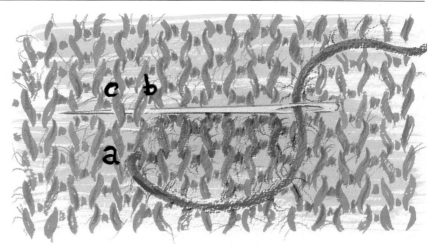

FINISHING

When many colours are used in a design, the darning in of loose ends after the knitting is finished can be dauntingly laborious. If you knit them in as you go by wrapping the ends around the main colour thread for two or three stitches beyond where they were last used, the job will be easier.

All garments should be blocked before being sewn up. Use a thick towel or blanket as a soft pad and pin out each piece of the garment to the correct measurements. If the fabric is textured (cabled or ribbed, for example) it should be lightly sprayed with water and left to dry naturally. But Fair Isle or other flat coloured patterns often benefit from a good press with a damp cloth.

Sew up using backstitch seams for joins which run parallel with rows (like shoulder seams). Invisible seams are ideal for joining two pieces of stocking stitch where the join runs at right angles to the rows (like side seams, for example).

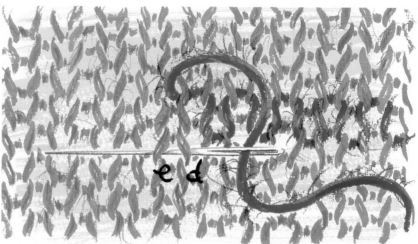

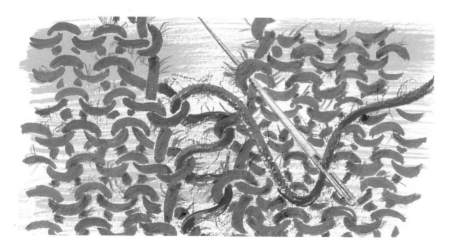

(Left) invisible seaming.

Abbreviations

alt – alternately	K – knit	rs – right side of work
approx – approximately	K up – pick up and knit	sl – slip
beg – begin(ning)	mm – millimetres	st(s) – stitches
cm – centimetre(s)	P – purl	st st – stocking stitch (stockinette stitch)
cont – continu(e)(ing)	patt – pattern	tbl – through back of loop(s)
dec – decreas(e)(ing)	psso – pass slipped stitch over	tog – together
foll – follow(s)(ing)	p2sso – pass 2 slipped stitches over	ws – wrong side of work
g – grams	rem – remain(s)(ing)	yfwd – yarn forward
in – inch(es)	rep – repeat(s)	

Hints for American Knitters

American knitters will have few problems in working from English patterns and vice versa. The following tables and glossaries should prove useful.

TERMINOLOGY

UK	US
cast off	bind off
catch down	tack down
double crochet	single crochet
stocking stitch	stockinette stitch
Swiss darning	duplicate stitch
tension	gauge

All other terms are the same in both countries

YARN EQUIVALENTS

The following table shows the approximate yarn equivalent in terms of thickness. However, it is always essential to check the tension of substitute yarns before buying enough for the whole garment.

UK	US
four-ply	sport
double knitting	knitting worsted
Aran-weight	fisherman
chunky	bulky

METRIC CONVERSION TABLES

Length (to the nearest ¼in)

weight (rounded up to the nearest ¼oz)

cm	in	cm	in	g	oz
1	½	55	21¾	25	1
2	¾	60	23½	50	2
3	1¼	65	25½	100	3¾
4	1½	70	27½	150	5½
5	2	75	29½	200	7¼
6	2½	80	31½	250	9
7	2¾	85	33½	300	10¾
8	3	90	35½	350	12½
9	3½	95	37½	400	14¼
10	4	100	39½	450	16
11	4¼	110	43½	500	17¾
12	4¾	120	47	550	19½
13	5	130	51¼	600	21¼
14	5½	140	55	650	23
15	6	150	59	700	24¾
16	6¼	160	63	750	26½
17	6¾	170	67	800	28¼
18	7	180	70¾	850	30
19	7½	190	74¾	900	31¾
20	8	200	78¾	950	33¾
25	9¾	210	82¾	1000	35½
30	11¾	220	86½	1200	42¼
35	13¾	230	90½	1400	49¼
40	15¾	240	94¼	1600	56½
45	17¾	250	98½	1800	63½
50	19¾	300	118	2000	70½

NEEDLE SIZE CONVERSION TABLES

The needle sizes given in the patterns are recommended starting points for making tension samples. The needle size actually used should that be that on which the stated tension is obtained.

Metric	US	Old UK
2mm	0	
	14	
2¼m	1	13
2½mm		
2¾mm	2	12
3mm		11
3¼mm	3	10
3½mm	4	
3¾mm	5	9
4mm	6	8
4½mm	7	7
5mm	8	6
5½mm	9	5
6mm	10	4
6½mm	10½	3
7mm		2
7½mm		1
8mm	11	0
9mm	13	00
10mm	15	000

Yarn Stockists

The original yarns used for these designs are listed opposite. In case of difficulty in obtaining the yarns, please contact the following distributors for lists of stockists:

ROWAN YARNS

UK
Rowan Yarns
Green Lane Mill
Holmfirth
West Yorkshire
England

USA
Westminster Trading
Corporation
5 Northern Boulevard
Amherst
New Hampshire 03031

Canada
Estelle Designs and Sales Ltd
Units 65/67
2220 Midland Avenue
Scarborough
Ontario MIP 3E6

Australia
Rowan (Australia)
191 Canterbury Road
Canterbury
Victoria 3126

Germany
Naturwolle Fritzsch
Gewebepark Dogelmuhle
D-6367 Karben 1

Denmark
Designer Garn
Aagade 3
Roerbaek
DK 9500 Hobro

Holland
Henk and Henrietta Beukers
Dorpsstraat 9
5327 AR
Hurwenen

New Zealand
John Q Goldingham Ltd
PO Box 45083
Epuni Railway
Lower Hutt

Norway
Eureka
PO Box 357
1401 Ski

Japan
Diakeito Co Ltd
1-5-23 Nakarsu Kita-Ku
Osaka 531

Sweden
Eva Wincent Gelinder
Wincent
Luntmakargatan 56 113
58 Stockholm

Italy
La Compagnia Dei Cotone
Via Mazzini 44
10123-Torino

Belgium
Hedera
Dietsestraat 172
B-3030 Leuven

Singapore
Classical Hobby House
1 Jin Anak Bukit
No B2-15
Bukit Timah Plaza
Singapore 2158

Mexico
Rebecca Pick Estambres Finos
Y Tejidos Finos S A De C V
San Francisco 352
Depto 202
C P 03100
Colonia Del Valle
Mexico 12 D F

Iceland
Stockurinn
Orlygsdottir
Kjorgardi
Laugavegi 159
101 Reykjavik

Finland
Helmi Vourelma-Oy
Vesijarven Katu 13
SF-15141 Lahti

JAEGER

UK
Jaeger Handknitting
McMullen Road
Darlington
Co Durham DL 1 1YH
England

DESIGNER YARNS

UK
Designer Yarns
PO Box 18
Longcroft
Keighley
Yorkshire BD21 5AU
England

BROCKWELL WOOLS

UK
Brockwell Wools
Stansfield Mill
Standlfield Mill Lane
Triangle
Sowerby Bridge
West Yorkshire HX6 3LZ
England

Knitting Kits

Yarn kits are available for the following designs:

Oriental Poppies – cream (page 12)
Anemones cardigan – cream (page 16)
Anemones jacket – black (page 20)
Red Roses – bark (page 24)
Hollyhocks – cream (page 28)
Indian Weave cardigan (page 34)
Indian Weave waistcoat (page 38)
*Tartan Flower jacket (page 42)
Tartan Flower waistcoat (page 46)
Wavy Fair Isle cardigan (page 50)
Wavy Fair Isle sweater (page 54)
Navajo cardigan – oyster (page 57)
Climbing Roses sweater – cream (page 64)
Orange Blossom cardigan – charcoal (page 70)
Brocade cardigan (page 76)
Auriculas cardigan – cream (page 84)
Auriculas sweater (page 90)

Chevron Floral (page 94)
Flower Vases (page 100)
Patchwork (page 104)
*Tapestry (page 110)
Rowan Berries (page 114)
Ivy Leaves (page 117)
Flower Wheels pullover – clove (page 122)
Rose Trellis (page 126)
Flower Tiles pullover – blue (page 130)

For information about kits marked * contact
Rowan Yarns, Green Lane Mill, Holmfirth, West
Yorkshire, England (or other national distributors).
For information about all other kits, contact
Knitting Kits, PO Box 1, Farnham, Surrey GU9 8UX,
England.

Note: In some cases the yarn shade supplied may not
match exactly the colour in the photograph.

Original Yarns

Note: Rowan DK Wool is a lightweight wool that knits in these designs as 4-ply. Merc. = Mercerized.

ORIENTAL POPPIES – Cream Colourway

A	Rowan Silkstones Silk & Wool	837	natural
B	Rowan DK Wool	101	cypress
C	Rowan DK Wool	93	deep lilac
D	Rowan DK Wool	19	sugar pink
E	Rowan Botany Wool	118	aubergine
F	Rowan DK Wool	43	bright fuchsia
G	Rowan DK Wool	92	strawberry mousse
H	Rowan DK Wool	14	gold
J	Designer Yarns 4-ply Merino	37	old rose
L	Rowan Edina Ronay Silk & Wool	842	red
M	Rowan DK Wool	122	loden
N	Rowan DK Wool	68	pale pink
Q	Rowan DK Wool	69	grape
R	Rowan DK Wool	46	claret

ANEMONES – Cream Cardigan

A	Rowan Merc. Cotton 4 ply	301	natural
B	Rowan Merc. Cotton 4 ply	306	blue scan
C	Rowan Merc. Cotton 4 ply	329	khaki
D	Brockwell Merc. Cotton 4 ply	474	flame
E	Brockwell Merc. Cotton 4 ply	475	red
F	Rowan Merc. Cotton 4 ply	326	cerise
G	Rowan Merc. Cotton 4 ply	312	wild rose
H	Rowan Merc. Cotton 4 ply	319	black
J	Brockwell Merc. Cotton 4 ply	487	battleship
L	Brockwell Merc. Cotton 4 ply	484	sage
M	Brockwell Plain Cotton 4 ply	516	lavender blue
N	Brockwell Plain Cotton 4 ply	547	purple
Q	Rowan Merc. Cotton 4 ply	338	geranium
R	Brockwell Merc. Cotton 4 ply	470	bengal pink
S	Rowan Merc. Cotton 4 ply	322	fuchsia
T	Brockwell Merc. Cotton 4 ply	461	pale lilac
U	Rowan Soft Cotton	542	bluebell
V	Rowan Merc. Cotton 4 ply	311	pale mauve

ANEMONES – Black Jacket

A	Rowan Merc. Cotton 4 ply	319	black
B	Rowan Merc. Cotton 4 ply	329	khaki
C	Rowan Merc. Cotton 4 ply	312	wild rose
D	Brockwell Merc. Cotton 4 ply	470	bengal pink
E	Rowan Merc. Cotton 4 ply	311	pale mauve
F	Rowan Merc. Cotton 4 ply	315	claret
G	Brockwell Merc. Cotton 4 ply	487	battleship
H	Brockwell Merc. Cotton 4 ply	474	flame
J	Brockwell Merc. Cotton 4 ply	475	red
L	Brockwell Merc. Cotton 4 ply	476	wine
M	Rowan Merc. Cotton 4 ply	322	fuchsia
N	Brockwell Merc. Cotton 4 ply	484	sage
Q	Brockwell Plain Cotton 4 ply	516	lavender blue
R	Brockwell Plain Cotton 4 ply	547	purple
S	Rowan Merc. Cotton 4 ply	326	cerise
T	Rowan Soft Cotton 4 ply	542	bluebell
U	Brockwell Merc. Cotton 4 ply	461	pale lilac

RED ROSES – Bark Colourway

A	Jaeger Matchmaker 4 ply	728	bark
B	Rowan DK Wool	90	cypress
C	Rowan DK Wool	77	red rust
D	Rowan DK Wool	71	mahogany
E	Rowan DK Wool	100	sage
F	Rowan DK Wool	91	bottle
G	Rowan DK Wool	70	mulberry
H	Rowan DK Wool	66	coral
J	Rowan DK Wool	43	fuchsia

L	Rowan DK Wool	602	wine
M	Rowan DK Wool	46	claret
N	Rowan DK Wool	14	gold

HOLLYHOCKS – White Colourway

A	Rowan Merc. Cotton 4 ply	301	cream
B	Brockwell Merc. Cotton 4 ply	484	loden
C	Brockwell Plain Cotton 4 ply	513	raspberry
D	Rowan Merc. Cotton 4 ply	326	cerise
E	Rowan Merc. Cotton 4 ply	319	black
F	Rowan Merc. Cotton 4 ply	305	washed straw
G	Rowan Merc. Cotton 4 ply	322	blush
H	Rowan Merc. Cotton 4 ply	329	khaki
J	Rowan Soft Cotton 4 ply	544	lilac
L	Rowan Soft Cotton 4 ply	556	catmint
M	Rowan Soft Cotton 4 ply	542	bluebell
N	Rowan Soft Cotton 4 ply	543	purple
Q	Brockwell Merc. Cotton 4 ply	476	claret
R	Brockwell Merc. Cotton 4 ply	478	gold
S	Rowan Merc. Cotton 4 ply	311	pale mauve
T	Brockwell Merc. Cotton 4 ply	461	lilac

INDIAN WEAVE – Waistcoat

A	Jaeger Matchmaker 4 ply wool	695	burgundy
B	Rowan Botany Wool	631	bengal pink
C	Rowan DK Wool	50	jade
D	Rowan Botany Wool	118	aubergine
E	Rowan DK Wool	126	purple
F	Rowan Botany Wool	95	candy
G	Rowan Botany Wool	125	turquoise
H	Rowan Botany Wook	667	coral
J	Rowan Botany Wool	97	navy
L	Rowan Botany Wool	44	scarlet
M	Rowan DK Wool	5	wheat
N	Rowan Botany Wool	125	delphinium
Q	Rowan DK Wool	601	port
R	Designer Yarn Merino 4 ply	28	gold
S	Brockwell Botany Wool 4 ply	234	apricot
T	Rowan Botany Wool	62	black

INDIAN WEAVE – Cardigan

A	Brockwell Merc. Cotton 4 ply	460	marshmallow
B	Rowan Merc. Cotton 4 ply	313	pastel peach
C	Rowan Soft Cotton 4 ply	523	wheat
D	Rowan Soft Cotton 4 ply	539	bermuda
E	Rowan Soft Cotton 4 ply	534	frolic
F	Rowan Soft Cotton 4 ply	533	antique pink
G	Rowan Soft Cotton 4 ply	535	sienna
H	Rowan Soft Cotton 4 ply	528	rain cloud
J	Brockwell Merc. Cotton 4 ply	455	cypress
L	Rowan Soft Cotton 4 ply	545	sugar pink
M	Rowan Soft Cotton 4 ply	542	bluebell
N	Rowan Merc. Cotton 4 ply	306	blue scan
Q	Rowan Merc. Cotton 4 ply	315	claret
R	Rowan Merc. Cotton 4 ply	330	navy
S	Rowan Merc. Cotton 4 ply	308	french blue
T	Rowan Merc. Cotton 4 ply	333	mauve pink
U	Rowan Soft Cotton 4 ply	527	smoke

TARTAN FLOWER-JACKET

A	Rowan DK Wool	62	black
B	Rowan DK Wool	9	ochre
C	Rowan DK Wool or angora	44	scarlet/red
D	Rowan DK Wool	128	lavender
E	Rowan DK Wool	129	charcoal
F	Rowan DK Wool	91	bottle
G	Rowan DK Wool	90	cypress
H	Rowan DK Wool	602	wine
J	Rowan DK Wool	14	chrome
L	Rowan DK Wool	41	fuchsia
M	Rowan DK Wool	100	sage
N	Rowan DK Wool	66	coral
Q	Rowan DK Wool	43	bright fuchsia

TARTAN FLOWER-WAISTCOAT

A	Rowan DK Wool	62	black
B	Rowan DK Wool	9	ochre
C	Rowan Edina Ronay Silk & Wool	842	scarlet/red
D	Brockwell Botany 4 ply	228	lavender
E	Designer Yarns Merino 4 ply		french blue
F	Rowan DK Wool	91	bottle
G	Rowan DK Wool	602	wine
H	Rowan DK Wool	92	strawberry mousse
J	Rowan DK Wool	41	fuchsia
L	Rowan DK Wool	90	cypress
M	Rowan DK Wool	43	bright fuchsia
N	Rowan DK Wool	66	bright coral

NAVAJO – Oyster Colourway

A	Rowan Merc. Cotton 4 ply	328	pale pink
B	Rowan Merc. Cotton 4 ply	308	french blue
C	Brockwell Plain Cotton 4 ply	534	turquoise
D	Rowan Soft Cotton 4 ply	533	antique pink
E	Rowan Soft. Cotton 4 ply	542	bluebell
F	Brockwell Merc. Cotton 4 ply	460	marshmallow
G	Rowan Merc. Cotton 4 ply	325	mushroom
H	Rowan Merc. Cotton 4 ply	312	wild rose
J	Rowan Soft Cotton 4 ply	527	smoke
L	Rowan Merc. Cotton 4 ply	313	pastel peach
M	Rowan Merc. Cotton 4 ply	305	washed straw
N	Rowan Merc. Cotton 4 ply	326	cerise
Q	Rowan Soft Cotton 4 ply	528	rain cloud
R	Rowan Merc. Cotton 4 ply	314	furnace
S	Rowan Soft Cotton 4 ply	535	siena
T	Rowan Merc. Cotton 4 ply	306	blue scan
U	Rowan Merc. Cotton 4 ply	311	pale mauve
V	Rowan Merc. Cotton 4 ply	304	jasmine
W	Rowan Soft Cotton 4 ply	523	wheat
X	Brockwell Merc. Cotton 4 ply	464	pale green
Y	Brockwell Plain Cotton 4 ply	513	blackberry

WAVY FAIR ISLE – Sweater and Cardigan

A	Jaeger Matchmaker 4 ply	698	navy
B	Rowan Botany Wool	118	aubergine
C	Designer Yarns Merino 4 ply	14	wine
D	Rowan DK Wool	89	lovat
E	Rowan DK Wook	100	cypress
F	Brockwell Botany Wool 4 ply	228	mauve
G	Rowan Botany Wool	127	buddleia
H	Rowan DK Wool	42	bright rowan
J	Rowan DK Wool	43	bright fuchsia
L	Brockwell Botany Wool 4 ply	212	ochre
M	Rowan Botany Wool	611	bright buddleia
N	Rowan DK Wool	426	gold
Q	Rowan DK Wool	141	fuchsia
R	Rowan DK Wool	142	orange tweed
S	Rowan DK Wool	67	rowan
T	Rowan DK Wool	65	petrol
U	Rowan DK Wool	57	royal
V	Rowan Fine Fleck Tweed	412	brick

CLIMBING ROSES – Cream Colourway

A	Rowan Edina Ronay Silk & Wool	857	ecru
B	Brockwell Botany Wool 4 ply	230	jade
C	Rowan DK Wool	62	black
D	Rowan DK Wool	100	cypress
E	Rowan DK Wool	68	strawberry
F	Rowan DK Wool	19	soft candy
G	Rowan Botany Wool	95	dark candy
H	Rowan Botany Wool	128	sugar pink
J	Rowan DK Wool	91	bottle
L	Rowan DK Wool	43	bright fuchsia
M	Rowan DK Wool	41	fuchsia
N	Brockwell Botany Wool 4 ply	228	aubergine

ORANGE BLOSSOM – Charcoal Colourway

A	Rowan Grainy Silk	802	crow
B	Designer Yarns Merino 4 ply	20	blue grey
C	Rowan DK Wool	88	blue green
D	Rowan DK Wool	25	bright apricot
E	Brockwell Botany Wool 4 ply	219	navy
F	Rowan Botany Wool	631	bengal
G	Rowan DK Wool	43	bright fuchsia
H	Rowan DK Wool	426	chrome
J	Rowan DK Wool	62	black
L	Rowan DK Wool	44	carmine

BROCADE – Cardigan

A	Rowan Merc. Cotton 4 ply	311	pale mauve
B	Brockwell Merc. Cotton 4 ply	455	cypress
C	Brockwell Merc. Cotton 4 ply	475	scarlet
D	Brockwell Merc. Cotton 4 ply	476	claret
E	Borckwell Merc. Cotton 4 ply	484	loden
F	Brockwell Merc. Cotton 4 ply	478	ochre
G	Brockwell Plain Cotton 4 ply	531	acid
H	Rowan Merc. Cotton 4 ply	310	rich purple
J	Rowan Merc. Cotton 4 ply	326	cerise
L	Brockwell Merc. Cotton 4 ply	471	royal
M	Rowan Soft Cotton	540	baize
N	Rowan Merc. Cotton 4 ply	470	bengal pink
Q	Brockwell Plain Cotton 4 ply	534	turquoise

BROCADE – Socks

A	Designer Yarns Merino 4 ply	19	smoke
B	Rowan Botany Wool	611	bright buddleia
C	Rowan Botany Wool	95	candy
D	Rowan Botany Wool	62	black
E	Rowan DK Wool	426	chrome
F	Rowan DK Wool	43	bright fuchsia
G	Rowan DK Wool	100	cypress
H	Rowan DK Wool	125	turquoise
J	Brockwell Botany 4 ply	205	coral
L	Designer Yarns Merino 4 ply	14	wine
M	Brockwell Botany 4 ply	230	cypress
N	Rowan Botany Wool	529	sherwood
Q	Rowan DK Wool	96	cerise
R	Brockwell Botany 4 ply	207	russet
S	Rowan DK Wool	68	pale pink

AURICULAS – Cream Cardigan

A	Rowan Merc. Cotton 4 ply	328	pale pink
B	Rowan Merc. Cotton 4 ply	313	pastel peach
C	Brockwell Merc. Cotton 4 ply	484	loden
D	Rowan Merc. Cotton 4 ply	326	cerise
E	Rowan Soft Cotton	556	cat mint
F	Rowan Soft Cotton	539	bermuda
G	Rowan Merc. Cotton 4 ply	336	saffron
H	Rowan Merc. Cotton 4 ply	315	claret
J	Rowan Soft Cotton	533	antique pink
L	Rowan Merc. Cotton 4 ply	329	khaki
M	Rowan Merc. Cotton 4 ply	330	navy
N	Brockwell Plain Cotton 4 ply	514	aubergine
Q	Rowan Merc. Cotton 4 ply	312	wild rose
R	Rowan Merc. Cotton 4 ply	308	french blue
S	Rowan Merc. Cotton 4 ply	311	pale mauve
T	Rowan Merc. Cotton 4 ply	310	rich purple
U	Brockwell Merc. Cotton 4 ply	477	mahogany

AURICULAS – Sweater

A	Jaeger Matchmaker 4 ply	681	black
B	Rowan Fine Fleck Tweed	62	black
C	Designer Yarns Merino 4 ply	24	blue pearl
D	Rowan DK Wool	40	green
E	Rowan DK Wool	129	charcoal
F	Rowan DK Wool	26	copper
G	Rowan DK Wool	426	ochre
H	Rowan Fine Fleck Tweed	90	blue green
J	Rowan DK Wool	69	dusty pink
L	Designers Yarns Merino 4 ply	20	blue grey
M	Rowan Botany Wool	95	black cherry
N	Rowan Botany Wool	118	lavender
Q	Brockwell Botany Wool 4 ply	234	apricot
R	Rowan DK Wool	95	candy
S	Rowan DK Wool	92	mauve
T	Rowan DK Wool	127	crocus
U	Rowan DK Wool	43	lipstick
V	Designer Yarns Merino 4 ply	37	old rose
W	Rowan Botany Wool	631	fuchsia
X	Rowan DK Wool	93	buddleia
Y	Rowan Fine Fleck Tweed	412	brick
Z	Rowan DK Wool	24	tan

CHEVRON FLORAL

A	Brockwell Merc. Cotton 4 ply	460	marshmallow
B	Brockwell Merc. Cotton 4 ply	464	peppermint
C	Rowan Merc. Cotton 4 ply	312	wild rose
D	Rowan Merc. Cotton 4 ply	305	washed straw
E	Brockwell Merc. Cotton 4 ply	478	gold
F	Rowan Merc. Cotton 4 ply	316	silver lining
G	Brockwell Merc. Cotton 4 ply	487	battleship
H	Rowan Soft Cotton	539	bermuda
J	Rowan Merc. Cotton 4 ply	313	pastel peach
L	Rowan Merc. Cotton 4 ply	315	claret
M	Rowan Merc. Cotton 4 ply	309	deep blue
N	Rowan Soft Cotton	542	bluebell
Q	Brockwell Plain Cotton 4 ply	534	turquoise
R	Brockwell Plain Cotton 4 ply	547	purple
S	Brockwell Merc. Cotton 4 ply	484	sage
T	Brockwell Merc. Cotton 4 ply	461	blue moon
U	Rowan Soft Cotton	533	antique pink
V	Rowan Merc. Cotton 4 ply	301	natural
W	Rowan Merc. Cotton 4 ply	326	cerise
X	Rowan Soft Cotton	535	siena
Y	Rowan Merc. Cotton 4 ply	304	jasmine
Z	Rowan Soft Cotton	556	cat mint
a	Brockwell Merc. Cotton 4 ply	470	bengal pink
b	Rowan Soft Cotton	534	frolic
d	Rowan Merc. Cotton 4 ply	306	blue scan
e	Rowan Merc. Cotton 4 ply	328	pale pink
f	Rowan Merc. Cotton 4 ply	329	khaki

FLOWER VASES

A	Rowan DK Wool	97	indigo
B	Designer Yarns Merino 4 ply	24	blue pearl
C	Rowan DK Wool	44	carmine
D	Brockwell Botany 4 ply	228	lavender
E	Rowan DK Wool	62	black
F	Designer Yarns Merino 4 ply	20	blue grey
G	Rowan Silkstones Silk & Wool	836	mulberry
H	Rowan DK Wool	94	garnet
J	Rowan DK Wool	129	battleship
L	Brockwell Botany 4 ply	224	red ochre
M	Rowan DK Wool	100	cypress
N	Rowan DK Wool	43	dark fuchsia
Q	Rowan DK Wool	142	range tweed
R	Designer Yarns Merino 4 ply	44	pine
S	Rowan DK Wool	128	blackberry
T	Rowan DK Wool	95	candy
U	Rowan DK Wool	41	fuchsia
V	Rowan DK Wool	426	gold
W	Rowan DK Wool	93	deep lilac
X	Rowan DK Wool	96	cerise
Y	Rowan DK Wool	69	grape
Z	Rowan DK Wool	125	turquoise
a	Rowan DK Wool	57	royal
b	Rowan DK Wool	121	mauve
d	Rowan Botany Wool	118	aubergine
e	Rowan DK Wool	602	wine

PATCHWORK

A	Rowan Botany Wool	602	Mahogany
B	Rowan Botany Wool	62	black
C	Rowan Botany Wool	102	mole
D	Rowan DK Wool	117	brown
E	Rowan DK Wool	129	battleship
F	Rowan DK Wool	604	deep claret
G	Rowan DK Wool	122	loden
H	Rowan DK Wool	620	ochre
J	Designer Yarns Merino 4 ply	44	pine
L	Rowan DK Wool	44	bright rowan
M	Rowan DK Wool	93	deep lilac
N	Rowan DK Wool	52	airforce blue
Q	Rowan DK Wool	78	tan
R	Designer Yarns Merino 4 ply	14	wine
S	Rowan DK Wool	69	grape
T	Rowan DK Wool	88	blue green
U	Rowan DK Wool	97	navy
V	Rowan DK Wool	70	mulberry
W	Rowan DK Wool	94	deep heather
X	Rowan Botany Wool	118	aubergine
Y	Rowan Botany Wool	100	cypress
Z	Rowan DK Wool	24	fox
a	Rowan DK Wool	46	claret
b	Rowan DK Wool	624	rose tweed
c	Designer Yarns Merino 4 ply	16	brick

TAPESTRY

A	Rowan DK Wool	99	clove
B	Rowan Fine Fleck Tweed	660	lichen
C	Rowan Fine Fleck Tweed	412	brick
D	Brockwell Botany Wool	224	mulberry
E	Rowan Botany Wool	77	red rust
F	Rowan Fine Fleck Tweed	44	red
G	Rowan DK Wool	46	claret
H	Rowan DK Wool	142	orange
J	Rowan DK Wool	94	deep lilac
L	Rowan DK Wool	26	copper
M	Rowan Botany Wool	45	rowan
N	Designer Yarns Merino 4 ply	44	pine
Q	Rowan DK Wool	128	strawberry mousse
R	Rowan DK Wool	62	black
S	Brockwell Botany Wool 4 ply	228	mauve
T	Rowan DK Wool	24	tan
U	Rowan Botany Wool 4 ply	118	aubergine
V	Rowan DK Wool	65	sage
W	Rowan Fine Fleck Tweed	12	citrus
X	Rowan Silkstones Silk & Wool	836	red ochre
Y	Rowan DK Wool	100	cypress
Z	Brockwell Botany Wool	225	win

IVY LEAVES

A	Rowan Silkstones Silk & Wool	833	marble
B	Rowan DK Wool	88	blue green
C	Brockwell Botany Wool 4 ply	207	red ochre
D	Rowan DK Wool	65	sage
E	Brockwell Botany Wool 4 ply	230	sherwood
F	Rowan DK Wool	91	bottle
G	Rowan Silkstones Silk & Wool	825	dried rose
H	Rowan Botany Wool	102	donkey

ROWAN BERRIES

A	Rowan Grainy Silk	812	blackcurrant
B	Rowan Silkstones Silk & Wool	825	dried rose
C	Brockwell Botany Wool 4 ply	230	cypress
D	Rowan DK Wool	88	storm blue
E	Rowan Fine Fleck Tweed	412	brick
F	Rowan Botany Wool	77	rust
G	Brockwell Botany Wool 4 ply	206	rowan
H	Rowan DK Wool	44	red
J	Rowan DK Wool	42	bright red
L	Brockwell Botany Wool 4 ply	224	red ochre
M	Designer Yarns Merino 4 ply	15	tan

FLOWER WHEELS – Clove Colourway

A	Rowan DK Wool	99	clove
B	Rowan DK Wool	128	blackberry
C	Rowan DK Wool	90	cypress
D	Rowan DK Wool	43	bright fuchsia
E	Rowan DK Wool	125	turquoise
F	Rowan DK Wool	426	chrome
G	Rowan DK Wool	95	candy
H	Rowan DK Wool	416	loden
J	Rowan DK Wool	66	fuchsia
L	Rowan DK Wool	126	purple

ROSE TRELLIS

A	Jaeger Matchmaker 4 ply	698	navy
B	Designer Yarns Merino 4 ply	20	blue grey
C	Brockwell Botany 4 ply	219	arabian
F	Rowan DK Wool	62	black
G	Brockwell Botany 4 ply	224	red ochre
H	Rowan DK Wool	129	battleship
J	Brockwell Botony 4 ply	230	sherwood
D	Rowan DK Wool	92	strawberry mousse
E	Rowan DK Wool	94	purple
L	Rowan DK Wool	68	pale pink
M	Rowan DK Wool	122	loden
N	Rowan DK Wool	41	fuchsia
Q	Rowan Botany Wool	501	buddleia
R	Rowan DK Wool	43	bright fuchsia

CLOCHE

A	Brockwell Botany 4 ply	219	arabian
B	Rowan DK Wool	46	claret
C	Brockwell Botany 4 ply	228	lavender
D	Brockwell Botany 4 ply	203	battleship
E	Rowan DK Wool	62	black
F	Brockwell Botany 4 ply	224	red ochre

FLOWER TILES – Blue Pullover

A	Rowan Grainy Silk	806	heather
B	Designer Yarns Merino 4 ply	48	cobalt
C	Rowan Fine Fleck Tweed	64	grey
D	Rowan DK Wool	429	lavender
E	Rowan DK Wool	48	pale blue
F	Rowan DK Wool	96	cerise
G	Rowan DK Wool	57	royal
H	Rowan DK Wool	126	purple
J	Rowan DK Wool	125	turquoise
L	Rowan DK Wool	14	chrome
M	Brockwell Botany 4 ply	228	mauve
N	Rowan Fine Fleck Tweed	666	rose
Q	Designer Yarns Merino 4 ply	19	pale grey
R	Rowan DK Wool	128	raspberry
S	Rowan DK Wool	66	fuchsia